Making It In America: Conversations With Successful Ethiopian American Entrepreneurs

AASBEA PUBLISHERS

Gebre, Peter Hagos

Making It In America:
Conversations With Successful Ethiopian American Entrepreneurs

Peter Hagos Gebre

ISBN 0-9703463-5-2

1. Ethiopian immigrant entrepreneurship
2. Immigrant Economic Adaptation
3. Business development
4. African Diaspora

I. Gebre, Peter, H.   II. Title.

ISBN 0-9703463-5-2 (Trade Paper)

Publisher:
AASBEA Publishers
All American Small Business Exporters Association, Inc.
2300 M Street, NW, Suite 800
Washington, DC 20037
Email: aasbea@aol.com
Web: WWW. AASBEA.com
Phone: (202) 332-5137
Fax: (202) 293-3083

Cover design and Graphic layout by Gene Hansen Creative Services, Chester, Maryland

Contents

FOREWORD

This timely book provides us with an anecdotal glimpse into the entrepreneurial spirit and nature of Ethiopian immigrants in the U.S. who are making psychological, sociological, and economic adjustments as the relatively new arrivals on the block. Although the year 2003 marked the centennial of diplomatic and people-to-people relations between Ethiopia and the U.S., it was not until the latter part of the 20th Century that we saw large numbers of Ethiopian immigrants arrive in the U.S., first as sojourners, who over time planted roots and became African Americans. Driven by diverse historical forces, they arrived in trickles in the late sixties and early seventies, and then in impressive numbers after the overthrow of Emperor Haile Selassie in 1974 by the military junta known as the infamous Derg. Today, the number of Ethiopians living in the U.S. has steadily grown and is estimated to be more than half a million.

Coming from all walks of life and representing most, if not, all ethnic groups of the ancient nation, these newcomers have settled comfortably throughout the 50 states with significant concentrations in the greater metropolitan areas of Washington, DC; Los Angeles, California; Seattle, Washington; Atlanta, Georgia; Dallas, Texas; Minneapolis, Minnesota; and Denver, Colorado. They brought their culture, language, churches, mosques, foods, costumes, spices, beverages, music, and dances. Wherever their concentration is great, "Little Ethiopias" are springing up flavoring their neighborhoods with a taste of the ancient land upon which the ancestors of man first walked. In Washington, DC for example, one has but to take a stroll down Eighteenth Street (lovingly called "Ginfile" after a river in Addis Ababa) in the Adams Morgan neighborhood on any given Saturday evening in order to be enveloped by the sound of the spoken languages, pulsating rhythms and pentatonic strains of music, and the enticing aroma of Ethiopian cuisine, all of which are now flowing down U Street on their way to enrich the Shaw neighborhood.

In writing "Making it in America," the author Peter Hagos Gebre gives us an intimate look into the thinking, and the hopes and aspirations of some of the immigrant entrepreneurs who serve as the engines that drive not only the commercial and industrial presence of Ethiopians in the USA, but also the revitalization and growth of the host of communities in which they work and live. The book is a small but important chapter in the history of the making of an Ethiopian Diaspora that has remarkably strong ties to the land of origin. The entrepreneurial success of these new comers is a reflection of genuine hard work and the great possibilities America has to offer. It is hoped that most of these successful entrepreneurs will, in due course, ask themselves, as they did in America, what they can do for their land of origin.

"Making it in America" is definitely inspirational reading and I hope that those who read it will be encouraged to follow in the footsteps of those who went before them.

Abiyi R. Ford, Professor
Howard University

ACKNOWLEDGMENTS

No work of this magnitude can be the result of an individual effort and this book is no different. Many people have been involved in the completion of this work and I would like to acknowledge their efforts and to express my deepest gratitude to them for their support and encouragement.

To Dr. Sharon Freeman, my partner and President of AASBEA Publishing, I would like to thank you for your unfailing support, contributions, counsel, and for publishing the book.

To Haile Kiros, Mengesha Wondaferaw, and Teklu Abraha who believed in what I was doing, and who helped me identify and secure the participation of some of the candidates for this book, I thank you. To the Abesha Group of young Ethiopian students at George Washington University who served as a sounding board to discuss the stories in this book and who raised questions and provided suggestions that were very constructive, I sincerely thank you.

To Sarah A. Carter for proof reading my work and for the valuable comments and suggestions she gave me, I wish to express my appreciation.

My deepest gratitude also goes to all of the interviewees in this book who made time in their busy schedules to be interviewed and to share their inspiring stories with the public. I would like to especially thank Zed Wondemu who was the first person who agreed to be interviewed for this book and who continued throughout the process to keep the embers burning in support of this initiative. I would also like to acknowledge and thank Geta Asfaw of Denver, Colorado for his support and for making me believe that I was on the right track with this initiative; his words of encouragement were particularly meaningful to me and helped give me the strength to carry

And to the readers, thank you for your interest in and support of the Ethiopian business community—your support matters.

I now invite you to walk a mile in their shoes.

About The Author

Peter Hagos Gebre was born and raised in Sebeya, in the Zalambessa area of Tigray, Ethiopia. He started out as a student in a Catholic seminary in Adigrat, however, wind the winds of social change began to blow, he blew with it, joined one of the opposition forces against the Derg regime, and became part of the younger generation advocating for social change.

Later, when the forces of social change were overwhelmed by the Derg's suppression, he decided to continue his studies at Addis Ababa University, where he majored in economics. He went on to obtain his Masters degree in International Trade and Finance from Lancaster University in the United Kingdom in 1991. He is currently pursuing a Ph.D. at Walden University in Applied Management and Decision Sciences, with a special emphasis on entrepreneurship development.

He began his professional career in the Government of Ethiopia in the Ministry of Planning and Economic Development, progressing up the ranks to the position of Head of the Macro Economic Planning Department, before his departure from Ethiopia in 1996. During his tenure he led several studies on the country's international trade policies, rules and regulations, and on regional economic integration. Consequently, he became a committed advocate and supporter of private sector led growth, and was one of the architect's of Ethiopia's first major private sector development strategies in 1994.

Since leaving the government after 11 years to join Lark-Horton Global Consulting in the U.S., like the other Ethiopians profiled in this book, he too has undergone a transformation, and in the process, has developed an even deeper appreciation for what it takes for the private sector to grow.

His areas of professional focus include trade facilitation, customs valuation, export strategy formulation and promotion, and private sector development. In addition to his work in policy areas, he also has hands on experience as an entrepreneur in America. His current entrepreneurial initiatives include an import and export business, through which he trades Sheba Secret™

Ethiopian spice, real estate investment, and business development consulting.

In addition to authoring, Mr. Gebre has recently formed the Ethiopian-American Chamber of Commerce to provide a vehicle and voice for Ethiopian entrepreneurs in the U.S., and to promote trade and investment between U.S. and Ethiopia. In writing this book, his goal is to cast a positive light of the role that entrepreneurship plays as an economic adaptation strategy for immigrants.

INTRODUCTION

T his book is about ordinary people who, through hard work, persistence, and entrepreneurship transformed their lives, and that of their families. Though form diverse ethnic, religious, family, and educational backgrounds they shared a common destiny of lives transformed through entrepreneurship. They also share a background of having started in America as first generation immigrants as waiters, parking lot attendants, taxi drivers, truck drivers, and janitors. Little by little, however, they saved money and started their own businesses to become trailblazers for their compatriots. As their dreams came true, they pulled up their families, friends, and many members of their communities by providing job opportunities in their businesses.

While the words entrepreneur and entrepreneurship can mean different things to different people, one thing is clear: The people profiled in this book are definitely entrepreneurs. Their examples provide a practical definition of what it means to be an entrepreneur. An entrepreneur is one who is able to see economic opportunities and transform them into businesses for economic gain. The stories in this book show what the entrepreneurs profiled in this book saw for themselves and how they turned their visions into business organizations.

Unquestionably, one of the distinctive features of America is that it is a land of opportunities. As a result, America has remained the center of gravity for those who dream big and who have the determination to make their dreams come true. Immigrants come from east to west and from north to south to try their hand as entrepreneurs. Ethiopians have joined the legions of immigrants before them who are making it in America. Although relatively new comers and small compared to other larger immigrant communities, Ethiopians in the United States have been making strides in academia, business, and in various professional fields. In the process they are contributing to the growth and prosperity of America.

This book, the first of its kind, is a collection of first-person interviews conducted with eleven Ethiopian American entrepreneurs whose stories not only show how they were able to succeed as entrepreneurs in America against the odds stacked against them; they also attest to the fact that in America, everyone has the opportunity to thrive as long as they have goals and work hard to make them come true. At the same time their stories give a picture of the hard work and discipline it takes to succeed in making one's dream come true. Many of the interviewees in this book had to take jobs beneath their academic preparation; yet, they stay motivated, and worked hard to improve their situations. They had to overcome language and cultural barriers and most had to rely on their own financial resources to start businesses, but they never gave up.

In candid, intimate interviews, they share their stories about their childhood, dreams, and role models, and about how they started their businesses. They also discuss the challenges they had to overcome and explain how they were able to stay in business when others failed; they reveal their sources of inspiration and motivation, and they share information about their current achievements, their future goals, and provide words of wisdom to emerging entrepreneurs on how to start a business and on how to thrive and strategize.

Their stories are relevant to anyone who is interested in demystifying the myth of entrepreneurship, particularly among immigrant entrepreneurs. Their stories are also particularly important for Ethiopian immigrants who have the dream to start their own businesses, as they provide an observational learning opportunity. Learning by observation is in fact the key distinguishing quality of human beings, and role models play pivotal roles in the process. The success and failures of others help us learn about what works best and minimizes the costs of learning by experiencing. If we were to limit our source of knowledge to our own trails and errors, the cost of learning would inevitably be too high.

I hope that by reading these stories many more Ethiopians will be motivated to pursue an entrepreneurial route for economic adaptation in America.

Why and How Ethiopians Came to America

Sometimes when the going gets tough, the tough have to get going, which in a nutshell explains why Ethiopians migrated to America. Unlike other immigrants to America in the 1970s, Ethiopians did not choose to come to America because of what they saw on television; in fact, some had never seen a television before arriving in America, and some didn't even have access to electricity. They didn't come to America to live a "Hollywood" life; they came in order to have a life and to have the basic freedoms that the American constitution secures for its citizens; freedoms they were denied at home. They came in droves at a time in the mid 1970s when a repressive regime had a stranglehold on their nation. Many were barely able to wrestle their heads from the noose to escape. They weren't planning on coming to America because their longstanding traditions and continuous culture provided a kind of security that money could not buy: They were happy in their homes. It is only when the situation became untenable at home that they had no choice but to depart from the cocoon of their lives that had taken 4,000 years to spin.

Before the turmoil of the 1974 revolution that *pushed* out many Ethiopians from their homes, most Ethiopians who came to America came to study and returned home. It is estimated that at the end of the 1960s, and early 1970s, less than 3,000 Ethiopians were in the United States, most of whom were on student visas (Metaferia & Shifferraw, 1991). From the mid-1970s until the mid 1990s, however, most Ethiopians came to the United States as refugees and asylees.

The Push Factors: Why Ethiopians Left Ethiopia

The mass immigration of Ethiopians to America began with the 1974 revolution, when the Derg regime replaced that of Emperor Haile Selassie's. Opposition to the new regime soon surfaced, starting with opposition from students, teachers, and workers that eventually took a more organized form. Clandestine organizations such as the Ethiopian People's Revolutionary Party (EPRP), the Tigrian People's Liberation Front (TPLF), the Ethiopian Democratic Union (EDU), and several other organizations sprung into action to oppose the tyranny. In response, the Derg took harsh measures to repress opposition forces, particularly aimed at eliminating the EPRP, which was becoming increasingly powerful in the cities and towns throughout the country. It is estimated that about 30,000 people lost their lives, excluding the deaths in war-torn areas of Ethiopia (Marina & Ottaway, 1978). Marina and Ottaway described the extent of the mass murder that had taken place in 1977, on the eve of May Day, as follows:

> Hundreds [EPRP sympathizers or alleged members] were arrested, taken to three different sites on the outskirts of Addis Ababa, and executed en masse. Scores of others were simply gunned down in the streets by the Derg's 'permanent secretaries.' Jeeps mounted with machine guns constantly patrolled the streets of Addis Ababa. The death toll may have been as high as one thousand. It was the largest mass execution of the revolution and marked the triumph of the 'red terror'. (Marina & David Ottaway, 1978, pp. 147-148)

Thousands of students, teachers, and workers suspected of being EPRP sympathizers were detained and tortured and many were killed. The Derg's methods of torture were particularly gruesome and prison conditions were extremely harsh. Citizens found that they did not have any legal protections and could be detained at any time without explanation or due process. Inevitably, the country plunged into civil war, which resulted in the displacement and emigration of hundreds of thousands of Ethiopians to neighboring countries and to the United States. At its peak, the number of Ethiopian refugees was estimated to have reached more than two million at the beginning of the 1980s. At the height of the civil war, the Derg also introduced mandatory national military service for students upon completion of high school. This was also a factor that contributed to mass exodus of Ethiopians.

On the economic front, land reform was perhaps the most important issue, with the popular slogan of "Land to the Tiller" as the rallying issue of Ethiopian students and intellectuals since the 1960s. Prior to the 1974 revolution Ethiopia had one of the most complex land tenure systems in the world, with several types of tenures coexisting in different parts of the county. The five main types of land tenure systems that existed pre-1975 land reform included: the *rist* system in which individual land holding derived from original founder or occupation of the land; *rist-gult* ownership of land as a result of inheritable grant made by the Emperor to the highest nobility or members of the royal house; *Semon* land in which the primary or reversionary interest is held by the Ethiopian Orthodox Church, and on which the church collects land-tax, tithe, and education tax; *Maderia* a piece of land granted by the government to its employees in lieu of salary or as a pension for a period of years; and *shehena* or *diesa* system where all land belongs to the village (Gilkse, 1975, pp.104-113).

Although according to Gilkse (1975), many aspects of the medieval land structure still exist, the post independence period witnessed a remarkable growth in private ownership of land and the emergence of real estate market. Private holding was most prevalent in the southern parts of Ethiopia so much so that holdings as big as 200,000 hectares were recorded for some areas.

When the Derg came to power, it placed all rural and urban land under state ownership and abolished the complex land holding systems that coexisted in the country for centuries. The problem for the Derg regime, however, was that it didn't have the resources and the capability to implement such massive land reform. The task of implementing the land reform program was relegated to high school students through a program called the *Development through Cooperation Campaign*, known as *Zemecha*. Beginning in early 1975, the Derg dispatched more than 50,000 students to the countryside to implement land reform and to carry out local development projects. Two of the interviewees in this book served in the *Zemecha*, which subsequently led them to join the anti-Derg forces.

Gradually, privately owned commercial farms, industrial plants, commercial transport, financial services, and real estate were nationalized and investment in most industry categories was reserved for the state; in addition, a ceiling of 500,000 Birr (US $57,800) was imposed on private investment. Instead of "power to the people," it was power to the government, which gained a stranglehold on the economy becoming its only investor and the single most important employer outside agriculture. Employment was centralized, as was the production and distribution of all goods and services. However, as in such other cases when the government displaces the private sector, similarly in Ethiopia, the government failed to create job opportunities to the ever-expanding labor force and created the conditions that pushed the younger generation to leave their country for greener pastures. Conditions were untenable, and in 1991 when the regime was finally toppled. Between 1981 and 1991, more than 18,000 Ethiopian refugees were granted permanent resident status in the United States compared to less than 1,400 in the previous decade.

The Pull Factors: Why and How Ethiopians Came to America

It is important to understand the immigration situation in America that enabled Ethiopians to enter the country. There are different immigration statuses and the interviewees in this book came to America under different immigration claims. A definition of the immigration process is given in Box 1.

Box 1: Definition of Immigrant, Refugee, and Asylee Status

What is an Immigrant?

Immigrants, as defined by United States immigration law, are persons lawfully admitted for permanent residence in the United States. United States law gives preferential immigration status to persons with a close family relationship with a United States citizen or legal permanent resident, persons with needed job skills, or persons who qualify as refugees.

What is a Refugee?

A refugee is an alien outside the United States who is unable or unwilling to return to his or her country of nationality because of persecution or a well-founded fear of persecution. Claims of persecution must be based on race, religion, nationality, membership in a particular social group, or political opinion. Persons within their country of nationality may be treated as refugees, provided that the President, after consultation with Congress, declares that they are of special humanitarian concern to the United States. To qualify for admission to the United States as a refugee, each applicant must meet all of the following criteria: be a refugee as set forth in the Refugee Act of 1980; be among the types of refugees determined to be of special humanitarian concern to the United States; be admissible under the Immigration and Nationality Act; and not be firmly resettled in any foreign country. Spouses and minor children of qualifying refugees also enter the United States as refugees, either accompanying or following to join the principal refugee.

What is an Asylee?

An asylee is an alien in the United States who is unable or unwilling to return to his or her country of nationality because of persecution or a well-founded fear of persecution. An asylee must meet the same criteria as a refugee; the only difference is the location of the person upon application—the potential asylee is in the United States or applying for admission at a port of entry, and the potential refugee is outside the United States.

Source: 1998 Statistical Year Book of the Immigration and Naturalization Services

Changes in United States immigration law over the years clearly facilitated the entry of refugees and asylees from Ethiopia and other countries. The 1965 Immigration Act abolished the national origins quota system, which favored immigrants of European origin, and established allocation of immigrant visas on a first come first served basis. Immigrants from Africa and other developing countries began to enter United States on the basis of worldwide quota allocated visa for immigrants. Another facilitating development was the 1980 United States Refugee Act, which established the procedures for allocation and admission of refugees to the United States. It established a comprehensive resettlement program for refugees, procedures for granting adjustment to permanent resident status of refugees and asylees, and procedures for responding to emergency refugee situations. By the 1980s, as a consequence, Ethiopia accounted for more than 87 percent of all refugees admitted to the United States from Africa.

The 1986 Immigration Reform and Control Act also provided another measure that changed the landscape for immigrants in the United States: It allowed illegal immigrants to adjust their immigration status to a legal one. Yet another milestone that contributed to the growth in the number of Ethiopian immigrants in the United States was the 1990 Immigration Act, which expanded the quota for family-sponsored immigrants and introduced Diversity Admission (DV) category beginning 1995. The latter category provides 55,000 visas per year globally. The visas are distributed among eligible countries through a lottery with a limit of 3,850 per country. As a result, the number of Ethiopian immigrants entering the United States through diversity program has taken the place of refugees and asylees as the primary enabling measure since the mid-1990s.

Based on the Immigration and Naturalization Services (INS) annual figures, the number of Ethiopian immigrants admitted to the United States has doubled from less than 4,000 a year in the early 1990s to more than 7,500 a year since the late 1990s. Ethiopia is currently the second country of origin after Nigeria for African immigrants in the United States. The three most populous countries in Africa: Nigeria, Ethiopia, and Egypt are three major countries of origin for African immigrants, as shown in Table 1.

Table 1: Ethiopian Immigrants Admitted in the 1980s and 1990s

	1986-1990	Total 1991-2002	1986-2002	% of Total
1. Nigeria	23,653	90,544	114,197	16.8
2. Ethiopia	15,189	67,935	83,124	12.3
3. Egypt	17,216	62,417	79,633	11.7
Africa Total	138,781	539,600	678,381	100.0

Source: Computed from 1998 and 2002 INS Statistical Year Book

The current estimate of Ethiopians (both immigrants and U.S. citizens) in the United States ranges from conservative 300,000 to more than half a million.

Ethiopian Immigrants' Patterns of Settlement In the United States

Ethiopian immigrants are found in many major metropolitan areas in the United States, from Los Angeles to New York and from Huston to Chicago, Ethiopian immigrants have settled in the suburbs and in major cities. Sixteen destinations have absorbed most Ethiopian immigrants, as shown in Table 2. However, Washington Metropolitan area in the East Coast and Los Angeles and the Bay Area in the West Coast are the two main geographic areas where Ethiopians immigrants are most concentrated.

While gravitating around major metropolitan areas, Ethiopian immigrants reside both in the cities and in the suburbs, and are dispersed throughout a broad range of selected zip codes. For instance, in the Washington metropolitan area, defined to include the District of Columbia; Arlington, Fairfax, Loudon, and Prince William counties and the cities of Alexandria, Fairfax, Falls Church, Manassas, and Manassas Park in Virginia; and Charles, Frederick, Montgomery, and Prince George's counties in Maryland, for instance, Ethiopian immigrants live in 147 zip codes out of the 258 zip codes surveyed. Yet there is some degree of concentration observed within these areas. In 25 of the 147 zip codes, there were 100 or more Ethiopians residing and in some areas, such as south Arlington and the Adams Morgan/Mount Pleasant area in Washington, more than 500 Ethiopians were found to reside (Singer, 2001). Such patterns of settlement seem to be common among Ethiopian immigrants in areas such as Los Angels, the Bay Area, and other cities as well.

Table 2. Estimates of Ethiopian Immigrants in the USA.

Major City/Metropolitan	Population	Major City/Metropolitan	Population
Washington Metropolitan Area (DC, MD,VA)	100,000	Boston, MA	10,000
Los Angeles, CA	30,000	Chicago, Il	10,000
Bay Area, CA	25,000	Columbus, OH	5,000
Seattle, WA	25,000	Huston, TX	5,000
Atlanta, GA	15,000	Philadelphia, PA	5,000
Dallas, TX	15,000	Las Vegas, NA	5,000
Minneapolis, MN	15,000	San Diego, CA	5,000
New York-New Jersey	15,000	Columbus, OH	5,000
Denver, CO	15,000	Indianapolis, IN	3,000

Sources: Compiled from various sources, including the Ethiopian Embassy in Washington D.C., estimates based on discussions with community leaders in some of the cities, as well as the author's own estimates.

Although dispersed throughout the cities wherever they reside, they have tended to create "Little Ethiopias" wherever they are. From establishing ethnic restaurants, groceries, sports clubs, churches, and community centers, Ethiopians have placed their marks on America. And while being Americans, they have also remained Ethiopians at heart. Metaferia and Shifferraw (1991) comment on how Ethiopians keep their culture intact noting:

> Ethiopians in the United States, especially where the community is large, are trying to maintain their culture through their foods; establishing churches; celebrating religious holidays such as Ethiopian New Year, Easter, and Christmas; and opening Ethiopian restaurants (although economic interests are also a consideration); by teaching the Ethiopian alphabets to their children; by establishing newspapers and journals in their language(s)... by listening to Ethiopian music [and radio stations]; as well as by being engaged in familiar sporting activities such as soccer games (p.76).

The growing number of Ethiopian churches in major cities and metropolitan areas are indications of the desire of Ethiopians to hold on to their institutions in their newly adopted home. In the Washington Metropolitan area alone, for instance, there are more than 15 churches; in California there are more than 10, and all together it is estimated that there are more than 40 such churches. In some parts church sponsored social organizations, known as *Mahabers*, also play important role in maintaining religious and social networking among Orthodox Christians. *Mahabers* generally consist of twelve members, who gather every month on their favorite Saint's day at their member's house to eat, drink, and socialize. Such *Mahabers* play positive role in nurturing their cultural and religious identity.

Community centers, civic organizations, and sport clubs also play important roles in keeping the community in tact and in helping newcomers get adjusted. Ethiopian community centers, for instance, are located in all major cities where there is large concentration of Ethiopians. The Ethiopian Soccer Foundation of North America is yet another organization that plays a pivotal role in bringing Ethiopian immigrants together every year. It is a significant organization in Ethiopian communities because every region in the United States with a sizeable Ethiopian population has its own soccer team and the Soccer Foundation organizes soccer tournaments in the different cities where there are large Ethiopian population. Not surprisingly therefore, the Annual soccer tournament has become an important forum for networking among Ethiopians. Political organizations, particularly in Washington Metropolitan areas, also play a role in bringing Ethiopians together, albeit, to a lesser degree, as most Ethiopians are increasingly focused on economic issues.

Making It In America

While some of the foundations to create a smooth social and economic adjustment to America are being laid by the various business, community, and cultural organizations of Ethiopian immigrants, it is also true that as new immigrant groups, many Ethiopians nevertheless have to face competitive disadvantages emanating from language and cultural barriers, lack of social capital in their new home, and at times, blatant discrimination.

For many, it has been impossible to find jobs in their field of study and some of the early arrivals in the United States found that their work experience and academic credentials have been devalued. In other cases, some found that there was a mismatch between their work experience and what the labor market demands, leaving them with no option but to take odd jobs and jobs for which they were over qualified.

It is not uncommon, for instance, to find Ethiopian medical doctors working as nurses or in drug stores because they had be to certified again in the United States in order to practice in their field. Many ex-government officials have had to work as parking lot attendants, as security guards, or driving taxis. In some of the parking service companies in the Washington metropolitan area, Ethiopian immigrants constitute up to 70 percent of their staff. Colonial Parking, based in Washington, DC, for instance, employs about 600 Ethiopians at various levels. The company's Operations Manager, who is an Ethiopian immigrant and business owner, is one of the subjects in this book.

Like earlier immigrant groups in America, the first wave of entrepreneurship among Ethiopians has been to establish businesses that cater to the needs of their own ethnic group. Not surprisingly as the number of Ethiopian immigrants have swelled, so have the number of businesses owned by Ethiopians to serve them such as grocery stores, restaurants and nightclubs, travel agencies, real estate agencies, car dealerships, law firms, and private clinics. In the Washington metropolitan area, for instance, the number of Ethiopian owned businesses have multiplied several times in the past ten years. There are more than 30 Ethiopian restaurants and about 40 groceries in the area, more than half of which are located in Washington, DC's "Little Ethiopia" of the Adams Morgan and U Street areas. Many of these restaurants organize live entertainment by Ethiopian singers, most of whom have come from Ethiopia.

In Los Angeles, "Little Ethiopia" has been formally named because of the many Ethiopian businesses that are located there on the 1000 block of South Fairfax Ave., between Olympic and Pico Avenues. Ethiopians have also made their mark in Dallas, Texas, and have created "Little Ethiopias" at the center of the East Dallas neighborhood, which extend for about two miles, and which include such Ethiopian businesses as grocery stores, tax services, nightclubs, garages, gas stations, hair salons, beauty supply shops, and video stores among others. Similarly there is a "Little Ethiopia" in Denver, where Ethiopians are fast cornering the liquor store market with more than 120 liquor stores currently owned by Ethiopian immigrants. In Atlanta, Georgia, Ethiopian immigrants are also staking a claim in business where they own gas stations and convenient stores.

Entrepreneurship Among Ethiopian Immigrants: A Closer Look

The subject of why and how immigrants start their own businesses is one that is gaining greater attention given the changing demographics in the United States. An often cited reason attributed to why immigrants go into business is the difficulty immigrants, particularly ethnic/racial minority groups, face in the primary labor market. The experience of many Ethiopians bears out the claim that discrimination, language barriers, restricted contact with the host population, devaluation of academic credentials for those who have studied outside the host country, and a lack familiarity with host institutions all play a role in creating barriers to assimilation among immigrants (Hosler, 1998).

The experience of Ethiopians in this book also shows that when faced with limited employment opportunities, many take the path of self-employment as a route toward upward mobility, just like other immigrants (Sanders & Nee, 1996). In other cases the emergence of new opportunities such as the rising demand for ethnic goods and services propels new immigrants into entrepreneurial action. "Selling exotic goods and services offers a fruitful path of business expansion because immigrants have a special product that only they can supply or, at the very least, present in conditions that are seemingly authentic" (Waldinger, Aldrich, & Ward, 1990, p.27). Ethnic restaurants are typical examples of such opportunities where entry barriers for non-immigrant entrepreneurs are considerable. People go to ethnic restaurants not only to eat, but also to experience the culture associated with it.

Ethiopian immigrants are also increasingly taking the path of entrepreneurship as a deliberate and concerted strategy for wealth creation, just as has been observed among Jewish, Japanese, Chinese, Korean, and other immigrants that came before them. And like Chinese and Korean immigrants, Ethiopians have also found that lending money to their fellow countrymen and women fills a need. Ethiopian immigrants use an *Iqoob* system, a rotating credit association, to raise capital for starting and expanding their businesses. One of the subjects in this book used an *Iqoob* to raise working capital when he started his liquor store in Denver.

Family support, both as a source of labor and financial resource, is yet another important factor for the success of many immigrant businesses. According to some studies family-owned businesses in the United States with no paid employees account for three-fourths of all immigrant enterprises (Sanders & Nee 1996; Light, et al. 1994). In many immigrant owned businesses family members own and run business together, in other cases, one family member owns the business while members of the family work full time or part time for it, thereby providing cheap labor to the owner, which helps the business to stay competitive. Because they have a greater stake in the success of the business, family workers also tend to be more productive than non-family labor when hourly wages are low. Most of the interviewees in this book relied on their families' support either by directly employing their family members, or by benefiting from indirect support of their family members.

Most importantly, however, personal attributes are believed to be the key to starting and succeeding in business. Among the commonly cited attributes of personal qualities of entrepreneurs are the individual's needs for achievement, independence, and risk-taking propensity (Brockhaus, 1989). These attributes are, however, important to any entrepreneur, immigrant or otherwise. The successful entrepreneurs included in this book demonstrate that to be successful, one has to have a higher drive for achievement; confidence in his/her ability to influence the outcome his/her actions, and to be tolerant of risk-taking.

Culture also matters and influences the extent to which society considers entrepreneurial activities such as risk taking, and independent thinking are encouraged. Hayton, George, and Zahra (2002) posit, "Cultures that value and reward entrepreneurial behavior promote a propensity to develop and introduce radical innovation, whereas cultures that reinforce conformity, group interests, and control over the future are not likely to show risk-taking and entrepreneurial behavior" (p.33).

In sharp contrast to the case in the United States where entrepreneurship is highly regarded, for centuries, entrepreneurship was looked down on in Ethiopia. Korten (1972), in his analysis of the pre-1974 Ethiopian social structure, for instance, pointed out that merchants and craftsmen had long been held in low repute in Ethiopia. Pankhurst (1990) also discussed how for centuries, most of trade in Ethiopia was dominated by Muslim merchants who "tended to be despised by the majority of population…"(p.207). Their dominance continued until the early 1970s. Not only was entrepreneurship looked down upon, some of the trades that might have formed a basis for future entrepreneurship were also shunned. For instance, blacksmiths were universally disdained despite the fact that they were responsible for the manufacture of wide ranging articles of considerable importance for the economy and military. They lived in constant danger of persecution and were not allowed to be part of the community so much so that they were even denied a Christian burial in some cases. While such cultural attitudes have been changing since the 1974 revolution, discrimination persists.

Such deep-rooted traditional beliefs and values systems undoubtedly stifled the emergence and growth of entrepreneurial class in Ethiopia before the 1974 revolution. As Korten (1972) aptly observed, there was little background to prepare an Ethiopian for entrepreneurship. "Most of the dominant Ethiopian groups, and the Amhara in particular, have remained content until very recent years to continue the tradition of leaving both the ownership and management of business enterprise to the foreign and the unfortunate"(p.32). When the Derg came to power in 1974, entrepreneurship was further stifled when the government abolished private ownership. The very small entrepreneurial class that had emerged during the 1950s and 1960s was abolished, and the government controlled the economy.

Despite the many barriers to entrepreneurship that have existed in Ethiopia, it has not been possible to completely squash the entrepreneurial spirit, especially among the Gurage ethnic group who are known for their entrepreneurial culture. Korten (1972) noted: "The Gurage's [are willing] to engage in manual labor, trade, and anything that provides opportunity to make money...[and] for this willingness, they have been subject to substantial discrimination by other Ethiopians. Unlike other depressed groups, however, the Gurage own their own land and dominate an important area of the country with which they retain their tradition" (p.40).

A recent study by Mengistea (2001) also showed that proportionally the Gurages have a higher rate of business ownership and performance relative compared to other ethnic groups. Furthermore, the rate of business ownership is far higher for the Gurage than for any other group. The Gurage constitute less than 5 percent of the labor force of the region from which the data were collected, yet nearly a third of the businesses in the sample were Gurage-owned. With a share of 40 percent of establishments, the Amhara, rather than the Gurage, constitute the largest ethnic group of business owners in the sample. However, the share of the Amhara in the regional workforce is of the same order of magnitude. Consequently, the rate of business ownership of the Amhara is far smaller than that of the Gurage, as is that of other ethnic groups. (pp. 3-4)

Today, however, entrepreneurship is spreading among different ethnic groups in Ethiopia, indicating a positive socio-cultural change and that entrepreneurship is regarded more highly in recent years. In the United States, a growing number of Ethiopian immigrants are joining the emerging entrepreneurial class, and some are even giving up their white collar jobs, which provides further evidence that entrepreneurship is firmly taking root among Ethiopians.

The entrepreneurs profiled in this book come from diverse social, ethnic, and geographic backgrounds in Ethiopia. They are Amharas, Gurages, Oromo, Tigrians, Christians and Muslims, and males and females. What they have in common is that none of them planned to live in America but once here; they made the best of it and embraced the American tradition of entrepreneurship.

Whether raised in small towns and villages or in the bustling capital city of Addis Ababa, what they also have in common is an uncommon desire and determination to succeed in life. Some embraced entrepreneurship early in their stay in America while it took others years to come to the realization that entrepreneurship would provide the means to the end that they sought.

All, however, realized that a road is a means to get somewhere; it is not a destination. Their destination, to move up through the economic and social ladder, to give back to their communities, and to retain their identities in a foreign land, is virtually the same for all despite the many twists and turns on their respective entrepreneurial paths. No matter what individual roads they may have taken, a strong motivation to succeed, clear goals, a greater propensity to save, and a high degree of persistence and commitment characterized their journeys.

The interviewees in this book also share another common trait: community involvement, and a continued sense of identity as Ethiopians. They have blended their worlds by creating "Little Ethiopias" in their communities.

Now, it is time to walk a mile in their shoes. As you read their stories, you will notice that each one of the subjects are referred to by their first names, which is consistent with Ethiopian practice. For instance, the first story is about Mr. Kahsay Abraha, and the author has referred to him simply Kahsay, instead of Mr. Abraha, or Abraha, as would typically be the case in other literary works.

A TALE OF TWO BROTHERS

This is a tale of two brothers who were born in a little hamlet in the north of Ethiopia. While they didn't have access to most modern conveniences, they were loved and full of hope. This story is essentially about how you can move mountains with a mustard seed of hope, as the success of the two brothers made who made it in America against all odds shows. The first story is about the younger brother, Kahsay Abraha, who is the owner of three businesses in Denver: Wadsworth Liquor & Wine, U Payless Liquor & Wine, and Jani-King Cleaning. The second story is about Teklu Abraha, the elder brother who is currently engaged in real estate and retail businesses in Denver.

Kahsay Abraha
CEO
Wadsworth Liquor & Wine and Jani-King Cleaning
Denver, Colorado

Kahsay Abraha was born in 1967 in Wootafa, a small hamlet with a population of less than 200, near the town of Adigrat in Tigray. He had to travel 20 miles everyday on foot to attend school. He also had to earn the money to pay for his schooling, which was no small feat given that there was no modern industry in the town and no readily available jobs. Kahsay had to create a job for himself based on his own ingenuity and drive. These assets, ingenuity and drive, would also come in handy later in life and enable him to become a successful entrepreneur in America who, today, travels in a Land Rover Discovery as he navigates between his liquor stores and his other business: Jani-King Cleaning, a franchise cleaning business. Between these two businesses, which he established in 1998, he employs seven workers, and has gross receipts over a million dollars per year.

Before he could get to America in 1991 he was himself a land rover, discovering every inch of territory between his home and his school. He roved over the rivers and through the woods not by bus, car, or even by mule: He had to walk on foot, without shoes. Once his classes ended he had to rush back home before it got too dark to cross the ravines, rivers, and streams that dotted the terrain. To make good use of his time on the long journey back home, he stopped occasionally to read his notes from the lessons of the day. He could have made his life easier by staying with his sister who lived between his home and his school but he didn't want to do that because he was so close to his mother that he didn't want to spend one night away from her.

Many of the things that Americans take for granted, such as access to power, telecommunications, transportation and to other infrastructural resources, weren't available in the rural area where Kahsay was raised. Kahsay didn't even have easy access to fire. In fact, one of the few ways in which he could earn money to buy his lunch for school was by finding and re-selling charcoal briquettes to households in the neighborhood that needed them for cooking.

Making Money

Making money was not a joke to Kahsay; it was about survival. From the time of his first consciousness he realized that he had to make money to survive. From selling charcoal to farming, he blossomed into a junior entrepreneur by the time he was 13 years old. He even helped support his family through the proceeds of his small agricultural plot. His first entrepreneurial endeavor was launched when he spotted a business opportunity to lease small plots of agricultural land in sharecropping arrangements with elderly people and widows who didn't have anyone to farm their land.

His little business was a winner and enabled him to buy clothes, textbooks, support his family, and have a little "walking around" money in his pocket. Kahsay explained how his business worked. "During the school year I took a lease for irrigable plots in my village to grow vegetables; I grew potatoes, lettuce, tomatoes, chili pepper, and a few other crops." When they were ready for market, Kahsay explained, he carried all 60 pounds of them, on top of his head for 10 miles to Adigrat where he sold them on the open market, and this was all before going to school in the morning.

"This was my routine for eight years until I graduated from high school," Kahsay said. "I never had to ask my parents for money, but then again, they didn't have any money to give me anyway: To the contrary, it was I who gave them money," according to Kahsay.

Kahsay could endure a lot but it broke his heart when his mother passed away. He said: "It seemed that my world came to an end when I was fifteen years old and my mother died; it was a great loss to me because I loved her very much, and she was the family's anchor, and a strong source of inspiration and motivation to me."

Although his heart was broken, he had to press on and grow up even faster. As he said: "I was needed." Already harsh before his mother died, his world seemed even harsher upon his mother's passing. Kahsay found that he had even more responsibilities now that he longer had his mother. He said, "My father was in his seventies when my mother died and the responsibility for caring for him fell to me, the youngest, and only remaining child at home. My siblings, brother Teklu and my sister Abeba who lived in Addis Ababa also helped out financially to the best of their limited ability." It was clear to Kahsay that he needed a plan to move forward in life, so he decided to leave Ethiopia to work in Uganda, and later in Kenya, where he believed the grass was greener."

In Search of Greener Pastures

Everything comes at a cost and the cost of Kahsay's early entrepreneurship was that he received poor grades. Places at university in Ethiopia were limited and only those with the best grades were admitted. "This left me out in the cold, and indeed it was a cold world," Kahsay said. He added: "There were no job opportunities for a person like me and to make matters worse, a civil war was raging, especially in Northern Ethiopia where I lived." Kahsay's options were limited: He could either join the army or the guerrilla fighters that opposed the Mengistu regime, or he could leave the country. He chose the latter. Fortunately, his brother and sister who had lived in Addis Ababa moved to neighboring Kenya and Uganda, respectively, and therefore were able to give him a place to live, and to help him leave Ethiopia to join them. Kahsay said, "They were successful in getting me enrolled in a college in Kenya and sent me the necessary documents to facilitate my travel to Kenya."

Just because one has the documents to travel doesn't mean that the road on which one is traveling is well-constructed, however. In fact, Kahsay's exit from Ethiopia proved to be a harrowing experience. It took nine months to get his passport and exit visa, according to Kahsay, and at times, it appeared that he wouldn't ever be able to exit. The difficulty, explains Kahsay, was that in order to obtain a passport and travel documents, he had to get a letter of support from *kebele*, *woreda*, and *awraja* (precinct, county, and provincial administrative levels) government officials. If any of them refused to provide the necessary letters, he wouldn't have been able to obtain a passport and travel documents.

There were many reasons why the requested support may not have been given, Kahsay explains. One of the main stumbling blocks was that young people of all ages were being conscripted into the army, and he might have been required to join. "It was a living hell," Kahsay said.

In shedding further light on his experience, Kahsay noted, "In order to file my application for a passport, I had to travel to Addis Ababa, which was more than 600 miles away from home. I had never been to Addis Ababa before, and by the time I got there, my siblings had already emigrated to Kenya and Uganda, so I didn't have relatives with whom I could stay." His problems didn't end there. He further explained, "When I went to file my documents at the immigration office I was told to come back after a month, so I dutifully returned to Adigrat, only to have to return to Addis Ababa after a month. When I got there, I was told that my documents were incomplete and that I needed additional letters of support, this time stating that I was not involved in any political opposition against the government; I was also told that I needed a release from the national service duty in the military." Once again, he had to go back to Adigrat to get the new letters and to travel back yet again to Addis Ababa, for the third time. This time he was lucky: He was granted a passport and exit visa to leave for Kenya. That was the good news.

The bad news, according to Kahsay, was that when he returned to Adigrat to bid farewell to his family, he was detained by the local authorities who accused him of supporting anti-government political groups and of trying to escape from the country. It seemed that his problems were endless. He reports, "I was kept in jail for a month before my case was presented to the local court. At first, my case was included in with the list of those charged with serious political offenses, charges for which the accused were typically taken to Mekele for interrogation and torture. Fortunately, I was tipped off about what was coming next by a relative. He advised me to bribe one of the security officers to transfer my case to the local court. This bribe cost money, however, and I didn't have any. In the end, I was able to borrow the sum of 150 Birr (roughly equivalent to $75) to bribe to the security officer to take my case off the dockets and transfer it to the local court in Adigrat. If I had not done that I believe my life would have been over. To be charged of a political offense was a deadly crime at the time." Kahsay remembers many people who were detained for political charges never saw the light of the day again.

The Plot Thickens

Kahsay had to fight every step of the way to make his dream of leaving Ethiopia a reality. He explained further, "After a month, my case was finally heard at the court. As a part of his ruling the judge decided that I would have to limit my movements to the Adigrat area and not leave town under any circumstances, not even to go to my own home village 10 miles away. Worse yet, I was ordered to issue a bond for 10,000 Birr (roughly equivalent to $5,000, at the time) as a form of security. Obviously I did not have that kind of money if I couldn't even afford to pay a bribe of 150 Birr." Kahsay did have a little luck, however. He said, "One of my teachers, who was married to my cousin, Aregawi Tedla, used his house as collateral to issue the bond. Unbelievably, my case was then transferred to Mekele, which is more than 80 miles away from Adigrat, after I had been ordered to stay in the Adigrat area. This was becoming the theater of the absurd so I decided to bolt, to run away. I departed from Adigrat in the dark of night and traveled on foot for two days, covering over 80 miles, to arrive in Mekele. I could not use local transportation because I did not have an identification card or any documentation to prove that I was eligible to travel."

Just when things seemed to be at their lowest point, something good finally happened for Kahsay. As he tells the story, "I met my cousin in Mekele and explained my situation to him and asked for his help. He knew someone in the court system that could appeal directly to the judge who would handle my case. It was on Good Friday, an auspicious day, when I met the very judge at church. When I told him my story he was deeply moved by the injustices done to me and by the risks I had taken to arrive at his court. He decided then and there to examine my case in his office and he rendered a decision on the spot. He explained that his decision would be relayed to the local court in Adigrat and advised me to go back to receive the verdict from there. I went back to Adigrat in the same way I came to Mekele, under the cover of darkness, because I did not want to be charged with contempt of court. Once again I had to travel on foot for two days back to Adigrat. Finally, I was granted the right to leave Adigrat and to travel to Kenya." This entire episode took Kahsay nine months.

Refuge at Last

Finally free, Kahsay began his journey in Kenya; the year was 1988. He stayed with his brother Teklu, who was working in Mombassa as a freight forwarding agent. He only stayed with him for a short time, however, before moving on to Uganda where he stayed with his sister who had an import and export business. "After staying in Uganda for one year I applied for United Nations refugee status; it took two moths to go through the process," Kahsay recalls.

"Once I was accepted as a refugee, I was then eligible to apply for refugee status in other countries and the first thing I did was to apply to Australia for refugee status. I was told, however, that Australia had temporarily stopped accepting refugees. Next, I applied to the United States, around which time my brother Teklu had emigrated from Kenya to the United States." His brother's move came at a bad time because Kahsay developed asthma while living in Uganda and had to move back to Kenya to await the U.S. decision. This time his brother would not be there to help him.

The good is always mixed with the bad in Kahsay's story it seems. At this point, however, the good thing was that his sister still had an office in Kenya and was able to employ him as a forwarding agent. As Kahsay tells the story, "I also held down another job as a sales person for a minibus company in Nairobi, and earned income by providing my services to Ethiopians who were new arrivals in Kenya who needed help writing and filing their applications for refugee status. My work helped passed the time as I anxiously awaited the outcome of my own application. In 1991 the answer came, and for once, my luck changed for the better: I was granted refugee status in the U.S. and arrived in Denver in November 1991."

There Must be Another America

Big problems require big solutions, so naturally, Kahsay expected big things from America. As he said, "My image of America was that it was paradise. It is not that I was wrong entirely; however, what I misunderstood was the level of effort that has to be put into achieving one's dreams and I misjudged the speed at which dreams could come true. I thought getting an education and starting a business were easily achieved. I thought I could go to school and graduate quickly, and just as quickly become rich." In reality, his dream was simply to get everything he wanted so that he could be in a position to help his family back home.

Reality soon set in for Kahsay. When he arrived in Denver, he explained, "Things were completely different than I expected. To begin with, the snow was up to my knees and the cold weather was practically unbearable. Secondly, the economy was in recession at the time and there weren't many jobs available. I had to look for any kind of job that I could get to support myself. I had no car so I had to wait for buses in the cold for long stretches at a time in order to get around the city to look for a job. Making matters worse, I did not speak English fluently."

He finally got a job and it was a relatively good one. It was at a printing company and he was able to make reasonably good money, factoring in overtime pay and bonuses. But the good times didn't continue to roll: The business closed after a few months and he had to look for another job.

His second job was as a dishwasher for the airlines at the Denver airport. According to Kahsay, the dishwashing job was the toughest job he had ever done in his life. It was monotonous and backbreaking. He explained, "There was a very long conveyer belt coming from the lower level up to where the dishwashers stood in line to retrieve the dishes for cleaning. First you had to put them in the washing machine, and then they had to be placed on a conveyer belt and arranged in order. We were given a half an hour break for lunch but by the time the lunch break came, I was so exhausted I couldn't eat."

There is a bright side to everything and for Kahsay, it was that he was able to save enough money to purchase his first car first car for $1500. This was a real breakthrough. He never owned a car before so it gave him a great sense of pride, not only to own one, but also to have purchased one in America made it really special.

All That Glitters Is Not Gold

The good news was that he now owned a car; the bad news was that he now owned a car. The car expenses soon started to pile up: gas, garage fees, traffic tickets, all started to take a toll. Under the circumstances, Kahsay found that he needed a second job. 7-Eleven came to his rescue. As he explained, his routine consisted of working on his second job at 7-Eleven on the night shift after working all day washing dishes. He soon found out why they called the night shift the "the grave yard shift."

"One night right after I finished working and went home to sleep, my manager called me to ask me to urgently return to work because one of the employees did not show up for work," according to Kahsay. He didn't want to say no because he was so desperate for his job that he couldn't afford to lose it. He returned to work against his better judgment. "On my way there, I was driving half asleep and while waiting for a traffic light, at one of the stop lights, I lost control of my car because I had released the break and was hit by a big truck that threw me to the side of the road. I was treated on the spot and luckily I didn't sustain any major injuries, but my insurance company had to pay about thirty thousand dollars because it was my fault."

Where Was the Other America?

The America Kahsay was living in was not the one of his dreams. As he recalls, "I was so disillusioned with America at this point that I decided to go out there and find the "real" America. Was it in another state, I wondered? I went looking for it in Seattle, Washington, in Dallas, Texas, and in Washington, DC, but I couldn't find it. Surely it wasn't in Dallas, which was the hottest place I ever experienced. It wasn't in Seattle either—it couldn't be with that depressing weather. So, I decided to return to Denver and to make the best out of it. I started taking English and computer classes to improve my language proficiency, but I wasn't happy."

Despite his unhappiness, he had to press on. He said, "Once I got back into the studying mode I decided to go further and enrolled in the Community College of Denver in 1993. Although the college accepted my application I was told that I was not eligible for financial aid because my income bracket for the past year was above the maximum income limit. I was in a quandary: on the one hand, I needed to have time to study, and on the other, I needed to work more to earn money in order to go to school. I chose to study." Kahsay quit his previous two jobs and decided to hold only one job, in a parking lot. To his astonishment, he said, "despite the relatively low income of a parking lot attendant it was still too high to enable me to qualify for financial aid. Eventually I found that I had no choice but to get a second job to pay for my college tuition."

Kahsay was in a "Catch 22" situation: He needed two jobs to be able to afford to go to school, but only one job to have enough time to study. What he also needed was a new strategy. Kahsay decided to temporarily quit school, and to lower his income so that he could qualify for financial aid the next time he applied. As he recounts, "I got a job in a liquor store that was

Making It In America

owned by an Ethiopian, which turned out to be the best thing that ever happened to me. While working there, I learned about how liquor stores worked from the bottom up: how the inventory was stacked for display; how to order stock; and how to make profit in the business."

"After working in the liquor store for one year, I was finally able to get financial aid and resume my schooling," Kahsay said. However, he also found that he couldn't focus on school while working in a liquor store, so once again his strategy needed to be adjusted. This time, he decided to drive a taxi on weekends while going to school full time. "I drove a taxi for five years while going to school." His ultimate goal was to become a Pharmacist but his grades were not up to par and he wasn't admitted. This is where everything turned around for him: When he wasn't admitted into a pharmacy school, he decided to change his plan in life and become an entrepreneur.

On Becoming an Entrepreneur

Becoming an entrepreneur is more than a notion: It takes money and much more, as Kahsay soon found out. He explained, "When I decided to start my own business I had savings of only four thousand dollars. The good thing was that he had already purchased a condominium, with the help of his employer at the liquor store where he had worked. This person graciously served as a co-signor on his loan for his condo because Kahsay's salary was not high enough to qualify for the mortgage. Because he owned a condo, when he approached the bank for a loan to start his new business, he was able to offer his condominium as a collateral. He had a little disappointment at the bank, however. As he explained, "One of the banks promised to give me an equity loan of twenty thousand dollars, but after examining my credit history, a determination was made that I only qualified for sixteen thousand dollars."

Kahsay started out in business an under-capitalized position, but he had to make do—and there were a lot of things to do. The first thing he had to do was to apply for a liquor license from the Aurora City Council. As he notes, "The process took five months and I was granted the license in 1998." By the time he got the license, however, his limited capital had been significantly eroded because he had to draw on it to pay the monthly rent for the premises he leased, and to pay lawyers for the services they rendered in getting the licensing permit.

By this time, Kahsay was married and his financial situation put a lot of stress on his wife, he explains, who had to work for twelve hours daily to pay all the bills and expenses while Kahsay struggled to operate his new liquor store. According to Kahsay, "Once I opened the doors of the liquor store, my inventory was so low that I had to fill my shelves with empty boxes to cover up the shortage. At the same time, I was putting whatever money I was making back into the store to pay the monthly rent and to acquire inventory. At one point, I used my credit card to purchase $10,000 worth of inventory."

Desperately in need of capital, Kahsay tapped into to one of Ethiopia's cultural legacies, the *Iqoob*, which is a revolving fund scheme. The way the systems works, as Kahsay explains, "The members of the *Iqoob* raise a certain amount of money each week, anyone who wants to borrow the money to start a new business or expand an existing one can borrow the money on a no-interest basis. There is also a lottery system to bid on being the next person in line to be able to tap into the funds. The money has to be paid back within a six months or a year depending on the number of participants in the *Iqoob*. "We had ten members in our *Iqoob*. Each member was responsible for raising $200 every week and the proceeds would be lent to the borrower who won the number to be next in line to borrow. I didn't get the next number but fortunately, the person who got it switched places with me in light of my urgent need to finance my inventory," Kahsay said.

Once he hit his stride in his business, he established a good working relationship with his bank, which extended a line of credit to him, making it unnecessary for him to have to draw further on the *Iqoob* mechanism.

Location, Location, Location

After three years in business under his belt by 2000, Kahsay was ready to expand and to position himself in the right location. Having the right location for a liquor store is critical and getting the right location requires accessing the right information and having the right business strategy. "What was critical to my successfully bidding for the liquor store premises was having a solid business plan, which I had shared with the landlord." Kahsay said that the landlord was impressed enough to grant him the lease over the other bidders who were better financed and who had more connections than Kahsay. "Having the right location in turn enabled me to get preferential pricing for my inventory from the suppliers," Kahsay notes. He therefor underscores the importance of having a solid business plan when starting out and noted that his plan not only reflected the numbers; it reflected his drive and motivation. He said that it was prepared with the assistance of professionals, which included advice from lawyers and bankers. He adds, "I have learned that in business, it is important to ask the right people in order to get the right information and advice."

One of the steps Kahsay took in preparing his business plan was to seek advice on it from a loan officer at his bank. Accordingly, the loan officer reviewed the content and structure of the business plan and gave him some suggestions concerning his financial projections. Kahsay said, "I rewrote the plan based on his advice and once I did that, the bank gave me a letter of support stating that if I obtained the lease, the bank would be willing to provide me with required financing. I took my business plan and letter of support from the bank to the landlord. He was very impressed with my business plan, my financial sources, and with my experience."

Making it Work

The liquor store that Kahsay acquired had not been operating up to par, in the landlord's estimation; therefore, Kahsay's work was ahead of him to reinvigorate the store. As he explained, "I had to reorganize the whole business operation, redesign the internal layout of the store, and demolish old shelves and construct new ones, which took about four months." The next steps, as Kahsay explained, entailed developing a strategy for marketing the new store to both old and new customers. Kahsay organized a grand opening event that included free music, barbeque, and drinks for everyone who attended. Kahsay said, "I used the event to get to know the people in the neighborhood and to promote my business. The event was a success, especially since I brought in some of the big names in the liquor and beverage distribution to sponsor my event."

Behind the scenes a lot of work was going on as well. Even though Kahsay knew the liquor business from having worked in a liquor store before opening his own; nevertheless he thought it was important to have someone with a stronger background in the liquor business on board to guide him, so he hired a manager with over twenty years of experience. "With good management and qualified staff there was no way I could fail to bring back old customers and attract new ones," Kahsay said.

Light at the End of the Tunnel

Kahsay's plans and hard work began to pay off and he made his first profit after six months. "Within two years," Kahsay explains," I was operating at full capacity and was able to purchase an even bigger liquor store. My gross revenue from my liquor store is now around $1 million dollars a year, and we have four employees, three of whom are college graduates. My franchise cleaning business called *Jani-King Cleaning*, is also doing well: We clean office buildings and I have two employees in that operation."

Kahsay underscores that he would never have been able to succeed in business without the love and support of his wife, Haimanot, who has been by his side through thick and thin and who has been supportive in everyway, both financially and spiritually. He explains, "We got together when I went back home in 1995 to visit my family after seven years outside of Ethiopia. While I was there, my family members introduced me to my wife. I had known her when she was a little girl, but we were too young to think of any relationship at the time. When we met again the sparks flew and we quickly got married. The problem was that I could not bring her to America because I was not U.S. citizen at the time. A year elapsed before I obtained my U.S. citizenship and could bring my wife to America. Today, we have two wonderful daughters, Sarah and Helen, who are ages three and one respectively."

Always Another Mountain to Climb

"One thing I have learned about business is that it is very dynamic: You can never stand still and rest on your laurels," according to Kahsay. "Another thing I have learned since living in the U.S. is about the power of advertisement. This is not something that we put a lot of stock in back in Ethiopia. In America, however, without advertising, given the level of competition across all industries, no one can make it in business." He adds, "In my case, for instance, there are three liquor stores in each of the three shopping centers near my store. The competition is intense and we have to work very hard to keep our customers and to attract new ones. Advertisement is the key for us and I have tried many approaches including discount coupons, free ice, preferred customer cards in targeted areas, and advertisement in community newspapers." Kahsay believes that, on balance, his main advertisement is his ability to provide quality products in a customer friendly environment. As he says, "We strive to make our customers happy in our store, to give them choices, and most importantly, to give them value for their money." He further notes, "If a customer tells me that my price is too high, I offer to match my competitor's price, as long as the customer can produce a receipt showing me that the price for the same item was lower at another establishment. If the price was lower, I then sell the goods to the customer at half that price."

On Being Competitive

Price is only a part of competitiveness; quality is equally important, as Kahsay knows very well. He states, "Given the volume of choices and vendors in my business, it is imperative for me to be knowledgeable about all aspects of liquor so that I can offer the best quality products to customers. I am constantly educating myself about liquor and regularly take online courses. I also attend various wine tasting events, and strive to learn something new every day."

"Presentation is another important element in selling wine and liquor. It is not just about presenting the wine; it is also about presenting the staff in the store to give the right impression about their level of knowledge about the product, Kahsay notes. "Our appearance, the way we communicate, and the manner in which we respond to customers are very important aspects of our image," he adds. "Having quality products and competitive prices is important, but we must make our customers feel comfortable about our knowledge so they will take our advice on which ones to purchase. Customers have to believe that we know what we are talking about when it comes to the quality of your products." There is also a difference in selling wine as opposed to beer, Kahsay says. "When you discuss wine you have to know about the variety of grapes, the fermentation and production processes, and about the type of food that goes with different wines," otherwise, the customers may not value the store owner's suggestions about which wines to purchase for different occasions.

"Knowing the nature of the business is also important," Kahsay hastens to add. "It is extremely important in the liquor business to understand and comply with the federal, state, and local regulations," according to Kahsay. "Once, he says, one of my staff refused to sell liquor to a customer who had a Mexican identification card. Some days later the customer called my office and complained about how one of my employees had refused to sell him liquor even though he had a valid identification card. I queried my employee to ascertain why he had denied the customer when the customer had the appropriate identification. My employee told me that he didn't understand what the customer's identification card said and that he didn't want to understand Mexicans. I explained to my employee that as long as a person has a legitimate identification card, we are obliged to serve the person. I then fired the employee and made the customer aware of the measures I took in response to his call. Serving the wrong customers can also be a problem. For instance, serving under age customers, or failing to serve customers, can land a liquor storeowner in a lot of trouble; therefore, we must ensure that we have the proper procedures in place to avoid such mistakes."

It turns out, according to Kahsay, "that local officials had sent under age people to our store to check whether we are in compliance with the rules and regulations governing the liquor retail business. I learned about this firsthand when I received a 'thank you' letter from the local regulatory office for passing the test. The liquor business can be tricky, according to Kahsay: On the one hand you have to make sure that you are not discriminating against the wrong people, and on the other, you have to discriminate against others.

Navigating the Bumps in the Road

The bumps in the road are not always confined to business: You also have to keep yourself together mentally and spiritually in order to be strong for your business, according to Kahsay. He explains that when he was starting out, there were some disturbing things that happened to him in his life, but that he never let them daunt his spirits.

One issue Kahsay had to deal with in the "real" America was racism. He explained, "When I bought my condominium in a predominantly white area, my Ethiopian friends warned me to be careful because they feared that I would encounter racism. They were right. When I moved into my condominium someone from the neighborhood came in the dark of night and sawed the two sides of my car's mirrors off and left them on the ground; the second time I found the front glass of my car broken, which I reported to the police. Another incident took place when I a bought a new car: The four tires of my new car were cut open. It was very frustrating at the time but I did not want to give up easily. Again I reported the case to the police, and this time, the police took the case very seriously and started their investigation by going into the neighborhood asking the community it identify the culprit. Many people in the neighborhood were angry about what happened to me and were determined to identify the culprit. Within a matter of weeks the culprit was identified and persecuted."

Making It In America

The incident made Kahsay aware of the struggle against racism that has been going on in the United States. To educate himself, he started reading books about the struggle of African-Americans. He then compared the minor incidents that happened to him with the extent of racism African-Americans had endured in the past, and realized that his travails paled in comparison. Kahsay says, "While racism is out there I don't make generalizations. I take things as they come and judge each issue on its own merits. I have many white people whom I consider to be my friends. For instance, I have bankers, lawyers, and other professionals whom I met when I first started my business, and who have been very helpful and supportive of me, so much so, that some of them have become close friends," Kahsay explains.

Kahsay also tells the story of how one of his white friends helped him tremendously when he was just starting out. In fact, this friend lent him $50,000 dollars just on the basis of trust. The person believed in his friendship with Kahsay and signed a check for $50,000 on the spot, without a formal contract. "Only a real friend would do that," Kahsay says. Kahsay adds, however, "I am not saying racism does not exist, I just don't make wish to make generalizations about it and I don't think about it until I see it, at which time I deal with it through the appropriate means. One thing is for sure: I don't let it hold me back."

Lessons for the Novice

"There are many things I have learned as an entrepreneur and many things I am still learning, Kahsay says. He says it is clear, for instance, that information is key. "If you get the right information, you will have a solid foundation for moving forward and making decisions. To get the right information, you have to ask people who are knowledgeable know about the matter, but you should also verify the information you get through cross checking and research. At the end of the day, there is no substitute for doing one's homework."

An equally important ingredient for success is having experience in the business you want to start, Kahsay advises. One should gain experience by working in the type of business he or she wants to start before stating a business. According to Kahsay, "By working in the business before venturing into entrepreneurship, you not only get first hand experience about the nature of the business, you are not so dependent on your employees for information. A case in point is when I opened my liquor store and tried to work with newly installed software to manage my inventory: I did not have prior experience about the software and was totally dependent on my employees to manage the system for me. I was not comfortable in being totally dependent on my employee for my inventory management so I asked my assistant, who was the expert, to show me how the system works. Once he started teaching me about the software, I realized that if I wanted to know more about it, I would have to devote more time to studying it fully."

Kahsay took an unusual step: He temporarily relinquished his role as a manager, placing his assistant in that role in his stead until he learned the entire inventory management system. The process took about two months, he explained. "When I mastered the system I resumed the position of manager. Today, I can manage my inventory and make timely decisions without any hesitation. The main point is, if I don't know my business well, I cannot operate it successfully. Today, I can say that I am an expert in my business."

"I can also say that I am living the American dream—the real one."

Teklu Abraha
Entrepreneur-At-Large
Denver, Colorado

"I was the lucky older brother. Unlike my brother Kahsay I didn't have to walk 20 miles to school everyday. From the fifth grade on, I attended a Catholic boarding school, the seminary of The Immaculate Conception, where everything was provided. I didn't have to worry about food, books, or shelter while I was at school. However, after four years in the seminary, I decided to change schools in the 10th grade, as the purpose of the school was to prepare students for priesthood and I didn't believe that priesthood was my calling. By the time I joined the Agazi High School in 1972, a storm of discontent was brewing over the land. As discontent with Emperor Haile Selassie's regime grew, it became difficult to remain at school because of the frequent riots and growing student unrest. So, I went to live with my sister in Addis Ababa where I hoped to complete high school, but once again political upheaval intervened, and I was unable to complete high school on schedule."

A lot has happened between the time Teklu moved to Addis Ababa and now. He has tried many businesses in many different locations. Sometimes he has succeeded and sometimes he has failed but one thing is for sure: He has never given up, and he is not tired of trying. Today, he is winning. He recently sold his liquor store in Denver and bought commercial real estate where he has located his new convenient store.

It wasn't easy getting to where he is today. At 48, Teklu Abraha has fought in the jungles of Ethiopia against the former Derg regime; been incarcerated and tortured by the Derg because of his political views; escaped out of Ethiopia in the dark of night; and moved to Kenya where he established and closed a business before being hit by a car in an accident that almost cost him his life. By the time Teklu got to America in 1990, he had seen and been through a lot. Within a year in the United States he established a business and did well for five years until he decided to sell his business and return to Ethiopia in 1995. In Ethiopia, he started and ultimately closed another business—all before he was forty years old. For many people starting a business is risky, but for Teklu, "risk" is his middle name.

The Long and Winding Road

The problem started for Teklu in 1975 when the new Derg government was ushered into power through a coup. Teklu explains, "I was drafted into a new form of national service, the *Zemecha* campaign, that called upon all senior high school and university students to teach in the rural areas and to help implement the government's land reform programs. During my first year in the service, I served as a teacher and a school construction project coordinator in my home village. However, as the major forces of change kept pressing for democratic rights and for the formation of a democratically elected government, the new regime soon turned repressive and violent. Students, workers, and intellectuals who were suspected of harboring opposition against the government were detained arbitrarily and basic individual rights were violated indiscriminately. The more I saw of what was going on with the new military regime in power, the more I grew in opposition to it."

Teklu decided to join opposition forces that he believed represented his aspirations for his country. He said, "While I was still in the Zemecha, I joined the Ethiopian Peoples Revolutionary Party (EPRP), which was fighting to oust the Military Junta and to form a democratic government in Ethiopia." He further explained, "I worked as an underground operative to raise money, to recruit new members, and to distribute materials circulated by the party. However, the Derg was determined to suppress any form of opposition, and about one year after joining the EPRP, the word got out to government security officials in Adigrat that I had joined the EPRP and I was hauled in and detained in a military camp for six months.

While in detention, I was tortured several times in what they call the "Number 8" torturing technique: My arms were chained backwards, my legs were shackled, my mouth was filled with rags, and then I was hung on an iron bar upside down. Members of the security force came in randomly and called me from my cell to beat me for hours on end with an iron bar inside a plastic tube. This was the most torturous of all the methods they used to extract information out of alleged opposition members. They tortured me to get me to name EPRP members in my area. Despite the severe torture to which I was subjected, I held my ground and refused to give any information that would incriminate and expose my fellow underground comrades. When the "Number 8" method failed to yield the desired results, I was finally let go with a stern warning that I would be killed the next time."

After serving in the "army," and after enduring torture, Teklu was finally able to rejoin high school. No sooner than he got settled in however, he was tipped off that the government was coming back to arrest him again. Teklu didn't hang around waiting for that to happen, however. As he said, "Like my brother, though for different reasons, I too had to escape from Adigrat under the cover of darkness. It was a good thing that I was tipped off because indeed the next morning after I had escaped, security agents went to my high school to arrest me. As an underground operative I knew my life was in danger and that I couldn't live in the town anymore. Consequently, I joined the armed wing of EPRP, the Ethiopian Peoples Revolutionary Army (EPRA), and for the next three years, from 1977 to 1980, I fought against the Derg regime in Gondar and Tigray."

Once again, however, Teklu became disillusioned, but this time his disillusionment was with the EPRP. It had begun to fall apart from the top. "After all the sacrifices many of us made, and the struggle we had carried out to bring democratic change in our society, the collapse of our organization was a great shock to my comrades and I," he explains. "I spent the better part of my youth fighting for the cause and now it appeared that all of my sacrifices would go in vain. When the EPRP disintegrated in 1980, the government granted amnesty to those of us who surrendered. We were placed in a camp for three months for reorientation and political indoctrination and then released to join our families. I had to start life all over again from where I left off, so I went back to Addis Ababa to live with my sister and finally finished high school after years of so many detours."

A High School Diploma Does Not Lead to a High Life

"Finishing high school in 1981 was only a beginning; my grades permitted me to join college but my pocket book didn't," Teklu notes. "So, I had to get a job to support myself. The hard part was to find a job in a society that relied on contacts, and I didn't know anybody, wasn't connected to anyone, and didn't have any money. Luckily, after many trials I got a job, in 1982, as a tourist guide for a private tour company, the *Wonderland Tours*, a local tour guide and motel company in Addis Ababa. As a tour guide I interacted with tourists from the United States, and in fact, I found it to be quite interesting. My job was to take care of logistical needs and to guide the tourists through the historical sites in various parts of Ethiopia. The exposure to foreigners was very much welcomed and I learned a lot from them. I also became acquainted with some American firms that would play a role in my future. I worked, for instance, with Conrad Hirsch of *Sobic Mountain Expedition* of Los Angeles, California, who became my lifelong friend."

While with Wonderland Tours, Teklu received training in river running and became one of the best river runners in Ethiopia. River running is an all encompassing sport, which entails rowing and paddling rivers and mountain hiking. Tours also usually involve hot spring bathing, visiting tribal sites, and wild life parks. One of the most popular rivers for river running is the Omo river. Rising in the highlands southwest of the capital of Addis Ababa, the Omo courses south for almost 1,000 kilometers, but never reaches the sea. It is the sole feeder of Lake Turkana, East Africa's fourth largest lake, which it enters just above the Kenya border. For much of the Omo's length the river waters sustain prolific numbers of Nile crocodiles and hippos. This is all part of the excitement of river running.

Just when Teklu thought he had finally discovered his niche as a tour guide, the government nationalized all private tour companies and created the National Touring Operation (NTO). Teklu joined the NTO, but it didn't last. Soon, he had to plan yet another escape from the Derg. As Teklu explains, "Just as I was beginning to settle down, tyranny raised its ugly head and forced me into hiding once again. It turns out that just because I was working with an American, I was being accused of being a spy for the U.S. Central Intelligence Agency (CIA). When the new concern was raised, I began to fear for my life, especially given my tumultuous political background. I didn't believe I was a cat with nine lives, so I thought I had better save the one I had."

Fleeing is not easy when you don't have any money and Teklu had few options. As he tells it, "My only option was to take a river running assignment to Omo River to enable me to get close enough to the Kenyan border to escape by crossing over the border on foot. It was essential for the tourists to request me by name, which I managed to arrange, as I was already considered one of the best river runners in my organization. I took a group of 13 tourists on a river running tour to the Omo River and guided them as close as possible to the Kenyan border so I could then flee into Kenya on foot."

Teklu made sure that his plan was as tight as he could possibly make it. He left Addis Ababa with his tourists, business as usual. "My tourist group was with me for two weeks. Three days before the end of the tour, I wrote a note to my American friend Conrad, with whom I jointly lead the tourist group, asking him to take care of the tourists because I had to flee. That night in 1984, I escaped into Kenya after walking for six grueling hours through a jungle to Kibish, a Kenyan border patrol location. The forest was very dense and there were many wild animals including lions and hyenas. But the danger that these obstacles posed was a lot less than that posed by the Derg regime.

Kibish, a small border town, didn't have much to offer in terms of services for refugees like myself. I had no money and no resources whatsoever. Having explained my situation to the Kenyan boarder patrols, I begged them to let me stay at the police station until I figured out how to get to Nairobi. After two weeks in the police station I met some people who were going to Nairobi who, upon listening to my story, volunteered to take me there with them to the refugee camp in Nairobi. I stayed in the refugee camp for four months before I was granted a refugee status."

Having official status enabled Teklu to seek employment in Kenya. He found a job with a small forwarding company owned by an Ethiopian in Mombassa. He worked there for two and half months until he moved on to a bigger company that made him a better offer. "My new job was at a shipping and forwarding company, *Almeta IMPEX*. I was the section manager, and after six months, I was promoted to the position of general manager of the Mombassa branch. For the first time in my life, I started making good money." The good times continued to roll for Teklu over the next three years. He felt that his life was finally coming together.

Teklu continued to excel at his job, so much so that he was promoted to the manager of the entire freight-forwarding department of the company. Teklu traces the beginning of his entrepreneurial ventures to the time when he started managing this department. As he recounts, "This position put me in contact with exporting and importing companies and ignited the spark of my own entrepreneurship. As I began to develop a business network in Mombassa, I saw the opportunity to do my own business." One thing about Teklu is when he gets an idea he acts on it. His idea was to start a chicken farm business on the side; he supplied chickens to hotels and restaurants in Mombassa. Two years later he moved on to owning a shipping and forwarding company, *Temleg Clearing and Forwarding Agency*, with other partners. He managed his company for three years until he left Kenya to reside in the United States.

The Entrepreneurial Spark

Teklu's entrepreneurial spark didn't really start in Kenya. In fact, he was an entrepreneur back in Ethiopia when he was working as a tour guide. He recalls, "My monthly pay check was very low and yet I had to help my parents and siblings, so I had to find ways to supplement my income. I used to buy coffee, honey, and grain from the rural areas and sell them in Addis Ababa when I accompanied tourists. From Addis Ababa, I would take clothes, shoes, and detergent and sell them in the small towns and villages as we passed by. But if the spark was ignited through my small efforts in Ethiopia, I exploded into entrepreneurship in Kenya because its environment was so much enabling for the entrepreneur than Ethiopia's. For one thing, entrepreneurs were respected there.

"As in many other times in my life," Teklu said, "it seems that no sooner than I got on a roll something happens to throw me off track. This time it was a car accident. While I was working in Mombassa I had a car accident in which my right arm was broken and through which I sustained substantial injuries throughout my body. I remained in the hospital for over three months and was unable to move from my bed. After all of that it turns out that my arm was not properly set and after I was discharged I had to return to the hospital for another six months."

During his stay at the hospital Teklu depended on his business partners to "mind the store." But it was like a fox in the hen house. It became clear that his trust was misplaced and the people he thought were his friends turned out to be his enemies. "While I was out of it, my business partners and so called friend got totally into it—into my business and ripped me off," Teklu recalls. "The only thing that was left was my truck: My money was gone, my office equipment was gone, and everything I owned pertaining to my business was gone. From then on, I focused exclusively on my freight forwarding business, but somehow I lost my stride in that business and never made as much money in it. As I had sponsored my brother and a number of relatives from Ethiopia to join me in Kenya, my lost of income was also their lost. Escalating corruption in Kenya was also one of the factors that caused a general business turndown. Seeing the handwriting on the wall, I applied for refugee status in the United States, and it was granted. Once again, I prepared to start all over again."

America: Land of Opportunity?

Teklu came to the United States with great expectations. When he arrived in Denver, Colorado in 1990 with his wife, whom he married in Kenya, he was full of hope. Like his brother Kahsay who followed him a year later, Teklu hoped that everything would work out and that he would be successful in business once again. "Unfortunately," he states, "when I arrived, the U.S. economy was in a downturn, and the only jobs available were minimum wage jobs, which at the time paid less than $5.00 per hour. Coming from Kenya where I had successfully run my own businesses, it was unthinkable to consider stooping so low. It was not only a matter of pride: how would I support my wife and children on such wages?"

Teklu decided to get heavy truck driver's license because it was the only good paying job he could get with minimum entry barriers. He took six weeks training and then got a job at Schneider National Carriers as a heavy truck driver. At Schneider, Teklu was given an additional two weeks of training in Wisconsin on how to drive on snow after which he started traversing several states. "For the first few months," Teklu notes, "I really enjoyed the job, as it gave me an opportunity to see and learn America. The down side was that the job kept me away from home for most of the time, which placed a strain on my family situation. At the time, my wife was pregnant with our first son. As she was new to the country, leaving her alone continuously became unbearable. Finally, she asked me to choose between her and my job and I chose her; quit the job, and became a taxi driver. Driving a taxi was not a bad interim solution, it turns out. In fact, after driving a taxi for one year I was able to save enough money to start my own business."

It didn't take long for Teklu to figure out how to spot business opportunities in America. With his entrepreneurial experience in Kenya under his belt, he was confident in his entrepreneurial visions and talents.

Back in the Game

Teklu drove a taxi for about a year and was able to save seven thousand dollars, which he used as a seed capital to start a liquor store. Teklu said, "With seven thousand dollars in savings, and a five thousand dollars loan from a friend, I opened a liquor store in 1992. Owning a business at the time made me a pioneer among the Ethiopian immigrants in Denver. Ethiopians owned very few liquor stores at the time. By contrast, there are over 120 liquor stores owned by Ethiopians in Denver today. Business was good and I started to make real money. But I couldn't leave well enough alone," he hastens to add.

"The news back home was calling me, drawing me in, making me want to return. With the collapse of the Derg regime in Ethiopia, and with a new government in place, I felt that I had to go back and throw my hat in the ring to help stake a claim for the future.

I have always been passionate about my country's development, and this time it became irresistible. In 1995, I sold my liquor store and went back to Ethiopia to start a commercial farm. Most people don't realize that Ethiopia has vast arable and irrigable land and a diverse climate, which is conducive for growing all types of cereals, vegetables, fruits, and cash crops such as cotton, sesame seeds, and others. Not only did I want to make money; I also wanted to fight against hunger and starvation that plagues our country despite its natural endowments. As land is publicly owned, I put together a consortium to apply for a lease from the government for a commercial plot of land in Humera then in Asossa in the western parts of Ethiopia." Teklu explains his excitement and disappointment when he said: "We were confident that we would be able to start our business quickly, but we were wrong. Things had not changed that much or that quickly and it took three years to get the allocation. By the time we were given the lease we had lost considerable time, energy, income, and enthusiasm, and in the final analysis, we went broke."

Teklu is a person who would never gives up, however. So, he fell back on a business he knew: tourism. He said, "Through my previous network I was able to find a partner from the U.S., Conrad Hirsh, with whom I used to work as a tour guide in Ethiopia. By then he had started a tour operation in Kenya, so I partnered with him to start a travel agency in Addis Ababa. As my specialty had been river running, we focused on organizing river running tours on the Tekeze River, which is one of the major tributaries of the Nile River. Our first outing was a success. We had nine people from in our group and our tour proceeded from Lalibela to the Tekeze Bridge, which took 23 days. The business was running smoothly until a war broke out between Ethiopia and Eritrea in 1998. When the war escalated the tourism business died, and so did my hopes of success in that business."

Never one to give up, Teklu yet came up with yet another new business idea: A restaurant in Addis Ababa. He obtained a lease for the restaurant in a government owned building and started serving food and non-alcoholic beverages during weekdays and organized events on weekends. "I had more than 400 customers a day and business did very well for sometime until public safety became a concern in government buildings. Public properties became targets of terrorist acts and because my restaurant was inside a government owned building, the management told me that my restaurant was becoming a security risk and I had to close the business. Given the volume of customers patronizing the restaurant, the management didn't want to be held liable if anything happened to our customers." With that, another chapter in Teklu's life closed.

The Flame Dims

All of this did not bode well for Teklu's already fragile home life. As he recounts, "My wife had to support herself through this whole ordeal, which lasted four years, and by the time I returned home, there was no home. It was too late by then but I realized that I had made a big mistake in returning to Ethiopia without conducting the necessary study and preparation. I mistakenly thought things would be easy and that a positive enabling environment had been created merely by proclamation. The truth is, it takes a long time for reality to catch up with dreams. While it was true that the new government had made some very positive policy changes, the bureaucracy was still overwhelming. After giving it my all but failing nevertheless, I had no choice but to return to Denver. In retrospect I should have never sold my liquor store in Denver. There were many options at the time that I did not think about. I could have subleased the store, hired a manager, or asked my wife to run it. My failure to pursue these options was one of the biggest mistakes of my life."

Teklu returned to Denver a broken man. "There had been times during my ordeal in Ethiopia when I didn't have food to eat and was too ashamed to ask friends," he recalls. "I also didn't want to tell friends and family about the extent of my financial problems. Finally, I had to call my little brother, Kahsay, in Denver to ask him to send me a ticket to return to Denver. Whereas I used to take care of him, now he was taking care of me. By the time I returned, my clothes had worn out and so had my relationship with my wife. Our marriage was over and she had filed for divorce while I was gone, and worse yet; she took the kids with her and moved out of Denver. I don't think I could have sunk any lower; I was heartbroken. I didn't even know where my wife and kids had moved to and it took eight months to find them. Even my former friends in Denver shunned me. Anytime we met by accident they avoided me like the plague. Had it not been for my brother, Kahsay, I am not sure if I could have survived. He not only supported me financially, he continued to believe in me, which allowed me to continue to believe in myself. Gradually I came out of the darkness, and as I did, I vowed that I would not give up on trying to be a success in business. This time, I took real estate classes and obtained a real estate brokerage license and started working for a real estate company in Denver."

You Can't Keep a Good Man Down

With Teklu, where there is will, there is way. His younger brother helped him make a way as Teklu explains. "My brother Kahsay was my supporter and my friend. I lived in his house for about two years until I got on my feet again. I also borrowed $2,000 from him to buy a car. As I was putting my life back together, I began working in one of my friends' liquor store for $6 dollar an hour while I was taking real estate classes. What a come down: From liquor storeowner to working in a liquor store for minimum wage. But so it goes. I was proud when I got my real estate license and sold my first property, which coincidently was a liquor store. This little victory buoyed me on and gave me the courage and motivation to start life all over again. Little by little things started to fall into place and I was able to repay my brother the money he had lent me. What I needed now was a better plan, a clear goal, and to stay focused."

After a long and winding road, Teklu was back where he started. Once again, he owned a liquor store in Denver. This time, he only had two employees, but it was a start. As he puts it, "My store is not the biggest in the neighborhood but it is a start."

It wasn't easy to make a come back when so many people had written him off, but his strength comes from adversity and he have had a lot of adversity in his life. "There is one thing I know for sure after all of this: if you persist there will always be a light at the end of the tunnel. I am an external optimist and I am also an entrepreneur at heart, not always the most successful one, but a very persistent one. Persistence does not mean one shouldn't learn from one's mistakes, however, and I have learned from mine. One of the biggest ones I have consistently made is making decisions based on emotions. I now realize the wisdom of examining issues from various angles, and the value in sharing ideas with others before making decisions. Making decisions without sufficient information can cost a lot. As I go forward, I am proceeding with caution and am arming myself with as much information."

Before this story could be completed, Teklu sold his liquor store and bought commercial real estate property. To be sure, if there is a rainbow out there, Teklu will climb over it.

Amsale Geletu
President & CEO
PMS Parking
Baltimore, Maryland

orn in 1962 in Addis Ababa, Ethiopia, Amsale Geletu comes from a long line of entrepreneurs: Her parents, grandparents, cousins, and many of her relatives were entrepreneurs. Entrepreneurship was in her blood. Not surprisingly therefore, when she arrived in the U.S. in 1982 as a student, the first thing that came to her mind was how to start a business. She saw business opportunities all around her and couldn't wait to take the plunge into entrepreneurship.

She never doubted her ability to succeed in business and wasn't afraid to try. When she did try, her first attempt was unsuccessful, but that didn't dissuade her. She succeeded on her second attempt when she and her late husband struck upon a winning business: PMS Parking.

Today, PMS Parking manages 15 parking garages in Baltimore, and has recently been awarded a subcontract with a new partner, LAZ Parking, to manage the Metro Parks located in Maryland, Virginia, and Washington, DC. Amsale currently employs more than 70 staff and will add additional staff with her upcoming expansion.

It is noteworthy that Amsale has blazed a new trail as the only black female owner of parking service in the tri-state area of Maryland, Virginia, and Washington, DC. Not only did she achieve her own personal American dream; she has helped many others along the way to do the same.

Lessons for the Apprentice

Amsale was exposed to business from an early age. Her grandparents raised her and both were entrepreneurs. They showed her how business was done, and the images she saw from an early age are indelibly etched in her mind. She saw, for instance, how her grandfather mentored young entrepreneurs and relatives who came to him from the countryside, and how he trained them to work in his textile shop. She also gained an appreciation for what it takes to run a business and learned about the routine functions involved in a business, such as ordering supplies, setting prices, and bargaining with customers.

Given the extent of her family's participation in entrepreneurship, it is not surprising that Amsale is Gurage, which is an ethnic group that is arguably the most entrepreneurial of Ethiopia. They are known for their negotiating skills, business acumen, and also for keeping their business within the family through their well-developed mentoring and apprenticeship programs. An experienced businessperson, like Amsale's grandfather, would be expected to groom a series of younger budding entrepreneurs and to set them up in their own businesses, which would entail providing them with capital, guidance, market resources, and assistance to enable them to strike out on their own. Amsale's grandfather played this role and created a network of businesspersons with whom Amsale is still in touch today, she explains.

Amsale's grandparents were in the wholesale textile distribution business: They imported local fabrics of all types. It was a "real" family business and many relatives came from small towns to apprentice with her grandparents. Who was a relative and who was not is a question to which Amsale would never have an answer because everybody was treated like family.

Amsale's father was also in the family business and was mentored by his father before starting his textile distributorship business. While his father didn't expect his son to repay the loans he gave him, he did expect his son to follow tradition and to mentor others, according to Amsale.

The hustle and bustle of business dealings was exciting to Amsale, no matter how much hard work was involved. And she saw just how hard the work was from watching her grandfather rise at five o'clock every morning to start his day, and seeing him fix everything around him despite having servants who could do it. He was a hands-on manager, at home, and at work.

She wanted to emulate him but there was one snag: He didn't want her to work in the shop, or even to learn how to run a business. Like other Ethiopian elders at the time, his dream for his granddaughter was for her to become qualified in a "white collar" profession. It was just as well because business was becoming an increasingly risky profession in the changing political climate of the time.

When the political regime changed in 1974 and the socialist Derg took power, private ownership was frowned upon and ultimately squashed. But, they couldn't squash Amsale's dreams or the positive memories she had about business.

What Do You Want To Be When You Grow Up?

Little girls can have big dreams and Amsale had one of the biggest: She wanted to marry Emperor Haile Selassie. "Everybody hailed him as a great man, and treated him as if he was a God on earth, so I thought he would be a suitable husband for me," she recalls.

As Emperor Haile Selassie was being toppled from the throne, Amsale's family listened on the radio and it was as if someone in their own family had died. Their sadness was a reaction to the loss of a leader whom they admired and apprehension about what was to come. There is a saying: "Coming events cast their shadows before." Her family's greatest fears came true when they were dispossessed by the new regime of the assets they had created through years of hard work.

Amsale's family pulled together the funds to send her off to school in America where she would have an opportunity to thrive. A key motivation for sending her out of the country was to get her away from the grip of the socialist regime that had begun to conscript the youth into service.

Her family soon realized that leaving the country was no small feat; neither was getting to America. In order to receive permission to depart Ethiopia,

Amsale had to get a letter of support from the youth association of her *Kebele* (local administration) stating that she was not involved in anti-revolutionary activities. She implored the Chairman of her *Kebele* Youth Association to give her the required letter, but to no avail. She tried to go through the system, but when it failed to work for her, and her papers were not granted, she resorted to using family connections. Ironically, it was more difficult to obtain an exit visa from her own country than it was to be granted permission to enter the U.S.

In 1982, at the age of 20, Amsale did what so many of her age did: She left Ethiopia. She was granted a student visa to study in America. She was lucky because she had an uncle who lived in Baltimore with whom she could reside.

Much to her dismay, she wasn't thrilled about Baltimore. Like many young Ethiopians, Amsale's perception about the U.S. had been based on movies, inflated news reports, and on what relatives and friends who lived in the U.S. had claimed. Accounts reflecting the lavishness of life in America, it turns out, were greatly exaggerated. The photos sent from America to Ethiopia, were just that: A snapshot. They portrayed only one side of the story, which showed the abundance of everything in America.

When Ethiopians visit home, they typically take gifts to their relatives. Their ability to do this, suggests not only that they have been successful in America, but also, on the face of it, that it must be relatively easy to make it in America. Consequently, many Ethiopians immigrate to America believing that life is easy there and that they will easily be able to attain their goals. The reality, of course, is different, and it only takes a short time after one's arrival to separate myth from reality, Amsale stated.

The view of America that Amsale got by living in Baltimore was not the one she expected, so she decided to go in search of the America in her mind's eye. She had a cousin in New York whom she visited in search of the "real and better America." To her chagrin, she found that it wasn't in New York either, which she says was too hectic, congested, and complex.

Eventually she postponed her quest for the "real America" and decided instead to focus on her education. She first attended a community college and then transferred to Towson University in Baltimore, Maryland, from which she graduated in 1987 with an undergraduate degree in business management and accounting. She explains, "As I had to finance my tuition fees and other living expenses myself since my grandparents had lost their fortune, I had to work two jobs: one at a parking lot on weekends, and another at a drug store. This was a sobering experience, and one that helped me to develop a realistic view of America."

Gradually, Amsale began to get to know people in Baltimore, to understand the city's layout, and to appreciate the beauty and richness of the country as a whole. She noted, "I began to appreciate America for its greatest asset, its true form of democracy, where anyone can realize his or her own dream if they work hard and are smart enough to achieve it."

Working hard is one thing; working "smart" is another, however. Amsale decided early on that she wanted to work "smart."

Amsale got on "the money trail" very early in her American experience. She drew on the lessons she had learned about how the Gurages conducted business, and applied them to doing business in America. Through her hard work and ability to save, she was able to finance her education. She found something was missing, however: She needed to create a more balanced life. When she met her future husband while attending university, she learned what she had been missing.

Amsale found a partner with whom she could share her dreams. She recalls, "It didn't take long for my husband and I to know that we were meant for each other. We had a lot in common: We worked hard, believed in saving money, and had the same goal of starting our own businesses when we graduated."

In reflecting on her drive to become an entrepreneur, Amsale noted that her aspirations put her on a path that diverged from the hopes and expectations her grandparents had for her. They had wanted her to be a doctor or a lawyer but she was determined to be a businesswoman. As she says, "you can't fight your calling, and I truly believe it was my calling to become an entrepreneur."

Proving that a positive enabling environment is instrumental in encouraging entrepreneurship, as soon as Amsale settled into America she quickly began to realize that there were many opportunities to make money. As she put it, "My entrepreneurship leanings went into full bloom when I began to see many opportunities for making money in America. I saw people like Donald Trump taking the business world by storm and I noticed how he followed in the footsteps of his entrepreneurial father, and I wanted to do the same

Making It In America

thing. I was lucky that my husband felt the same way and was willing to enter into a business partnership with me."

Choosing a Business

"It is easy to say that you want to start a business, but how do you choose the right business to start? Amsale underscores. My then-fiancée and future husband, and I were split on the issue of which business to choose. We narrowed it down to two options: A restaurant or a parking business." Her fiancée favored the former and she favored the latter.

Amsale put forward the following argument to persuade her fiancée: He was already working as a manager in a parking company and I was working as a parking attendant, so as we knew the business, it would be easy to do that business. On the other hand, her fiancée' grew up in a family that had a successful restaurant business in Ethiopia, so he had that business model in mind.

In the end, Amsale's fiancée won out and in 1986 they opened a restaurant, together with another partner in Baltimore. The experience proved to be a testing ground in their relationship and in their partnership together," she says.

The good news, as Amsale explains, was that it appeared that her fiancée was right: Their Ethiopian restaurant started out very well. It caught the attention of local officials and the business community and they were offered free advertising in various media as part of an initiative to promote immigrant and minority businesses in Baltimore. The advertisements contributed to the success of the restaurant, she noted.

The good times did not continue to roll, however. Amsale explains, "For six months the restaurant did quite well, but then the partnership with the third party began to fall apart. In a nutshell, our partner did not have the same level of commitment to hard work as we did, so we dissolved the partnership and exited the restaurant business."

Amsale also noted that in the final analysis, the returns in the restaurant business, at least at their level, were not commensurate with the effort they put into it; they worked around the clock, seven days a week. When they finally closed the doors, they had lost money, though they had gained valuable lessons and experience, she said. They weren't wiped out financially, however; they still had enough money to start a new business.

Upon dissolving their restaurant business, Amsale and her fiancée' found time to think about their relationship and to make one of the most important decisions in their lives: To get married. They tied the knot in 1988.

A New Lease On Life

With one business down and a new marriage, it was time to start all over. This time, it would be in the parking business.

In order to identify an opportunity in the parking lot business, Amsale approached her former boss of the parking company where she previously worked and asked him for his suggestions. He knew about a great opportunity: A parking garage that wasn't being managed properly that the owner wanted to lease.

One of the problems with this deal was that a hefty insurance policy was required, one with a value of over one million dollars, Amsale explained. There were other requirements as well: new ticket machines, new cashier's booths, and new computer systems. Nevertheless, we decided to take the risk involved and raised the necessary investment funds. A few months after dissolving our first business and getting married, we were in the parking business: PMS Parking.

There are vital components of business that make any business a success; the parking business is no different. It is a business with its own complexities and challenges, just like other businesses. Amsale acknowledges, however, when they started out in the parking business as owners, rather than as employees, there was a lot for them to learn.

At the time, there were only three companies in Baltimore that managed the parking garages owned by the city. They had established a "good old boys" network, and whenever a new garage became available, they would control it, and divide the spoils amongst themselves, Amsale says. While it was hard to break through the "lockdown" they had on this business; it wasn't any harder than getting to America from Ethiopia in the first place, and it wasn't harder than working two jobs while going to university, Amsale is quick to add. As she said, "We were ready to fight the 'good old boy's network and to take our battle to City Hall. In the process, the old adage that 'you can't fight City Hall,' was proven wrong.

There were nine city-owned parking garages at the time that Amsale and her husband were looking to break through. Public bids to manage the garages were supposed to be held every five years, but they weren't. Amsale explained, "When garages under management were supposed to come up for bid, we approached the director of the city's owned garages to encourage him to open them up for bidding. He wasn't persuaded, however. Despite our pleading, he wouldn't open up the bids and at one point told us directly that, 'he was happy with the existing manager and didn't want to add any more.'"

For years, bids that were supposed to come out didn't; the few firms that had contracts to manage garages were thereby able to hold onto their contracts. Amsale and her husband continued to try, however. As she explained, "We challenged the director and tried to convince him that we understood the parking business and were worthy of consideration—for instance, we told him that we understood sources of inefficiency in the parking business and how to increase revenue by improving the management of the business, but he still wouldn't give us a chance to bid."

Amsale wasn't asking the director for a favor or grant; she was simply asking him to level the playing field. The prospects of changing the situation looked slim. As Amsale noted, anytime a parking director tells you that he doesn't want to increase revenue, there seems little hope of changing the status quo."

At their wits end, Amsale and her husband decided to visit the Minority Business Resource Center in Baltimore to seek their assistance. They explained to the staff what they had been through in the past two years with the city and sought their advice. The staff was very sympathetic to they plight and tried to help them by writing a letter to the parking director on their behalf, but they got the same response that Amsale had been getting.

At this point, the staff at the Resource Center advised Amsale and her husband to hire a lawyer to fight for their rights. They were referred to Elijah Cummings, who was practicing law in Baltimore at the time. (This was prior to his election as a State Delegate of Maryland and before his subsequent election to the U.S. Congress.)

Mr. Cummings queried them about the viability of their business plan for managing parking garages, attempting to ensure that they could, in fact, increase revenue for the city. "Since we were challenging a system that seemed to be working well, he wanted to make sure that he was dealing with credible and reliable business people and that our case had merit," Amsale explained. There were risks involved; "we hadn't established a long track record of managing parking garages," according to Amsale. But she added, "we had done our homework, we had over eight years of practical day-to-day experience working in the parking industry, and we knew what we were doing."

Once Mr. Cummings understood their situation he accepted their case. After doing his own investigation of the situation, he approached the parking director and tried to convince him to include Amsale and her husband on the bid list. "He set up a meeting between the parties with the director and pleaded the case in person. The response was negative and he observed firsthand that this system was not fair and that the director had no intention of changing the status quo," according to Amsale.

A heavier hand was needed. As Amsale recounts, "Mr. Cummings decided to take our case further, all the way to the Mayor's office and arranged for us to have an audience with him to enable us to plead our case directly with him," Amsale explained. The Mayor intervened and saw to it that Amsale and her husband were able to bid in the next go round. According to Amsale, it took her two years to get on the bid list and another year for her to win a bid.

Light at the End of the Tunnel

The light at the end of the tunnel came in 1991 when their names were finally placed on the bidding list. At the time, there were three public garages included in the bid package: a convention center parking lot; a hotel garage; and a stadium parking lot. Incredibly, Amsale and her husband won all three bids.

What distinguished Amsale's bid was her promise to either double the revenue stream or to withdraw from managing the garages.

This was a new approach and Amsale's competitors didn't like it. They complained that Amsale's wasn't a "real" company and that Amsale and her husband were foreigners and didn't know the parking business. They further criticized the proposed management fee and claimed that it was unrealistic and that they couldn't deliver what they had promised.

The proof was in the pudding, however. Amsale and her husband knew the stakes were high: "If we didn't deliver we stood to lose everything—years of hard work, our reputation, and future opportunities," Amsale said.

Amsale's goal was to double the revenue of the garages under her management in one year, and she achieved it. She also won another victory: The director who had denied them access to previous bids was forced to resign.

"Elijah Cummings, and others who had believed in and fought for us, were proud of our success and were also glad that they had 'backed the right horse,' Amsale notes.

Amsale and her husband, Getahun, weren't surprised that they won their bids. After all, they knew that the key to succeeding in the parking business was having a good management team, and they had one. In explaining the importance of having a solid management team, Amsale underscores: "You need a good management team to succeed in this business and employees must always know that you are on top of the situation. Paying attention to detail is key; you have to make sure that, at the end of the day, the garages are utilized to full capacity. To accomplish this, we hired three managers who had extensive experience in managing parking garages; the garages were operated around the clock, 24 hours a day, including holidays; and we put in the management systems required to enable us to manage the business effectively."

One key ingredient to Amsale's success in the parking business was to keep her eyes on the cash flow. As she states: "This is the single greatest challenge in the cash-based parking business." As most of the revenue is collected in cash, it is important to have a dependable and effective financial control system, she adds—and the key to such a system is to frequently upgrade the cash registering and dispensing system.

At the end of the day, however, there is no substitute for having trustworthy, dependable, and loyal employees, Amsale explains. In order to gain their loyalty, she says, you have to give them respect. "I work with our employees very closely and treat everyone as family members. Treating employees as family members is an example I learned from my grandfather." She also learned to mentor her employees and to have a network of referrals to new employees from existing ones.

Management style also matters, Amsale notes. Her style is to delegate authority. She explains, "I always share information and responsibilities, and in return, I expect full commitment to the job. I am also a strong believer in human resource development through training; all of my employees receive training before they commence their jobs." Amsale also ensures that existing employees are given many opportunities to upgrade their skills through training programs run by the International Parking Institute, and through cross-training arrangements with other companies. By getting training in other companies, Amsale explains, her employees get exposure to how other companies serve their customers and to how they solve day-to-day operational problems. The human touch is also important, because without it, you cannot gain loyalty and motivate people, Amsale says.

Her human touch has clearly paid off. She has been able to expand the scope of business from one to fifteen locations, and to do it almost exclusively with internal financing. That she is able to self-finance is one clear measure of her success. In fact, in fifteen years, she has only had to take out one loan for the expansion and upgrading of one of her garages. Even on that occasion, it was a matter of adding flexibility and convenience to her financial management, rather than a matter of necessity. "We started saving money from the very beginning," she notes. Because the city provided a two-month advance management fee at the time, she was able to build their cash flow and manage their overhead expenses at the same time, she adds.

Today, PMS Parking Inc. manages the majority of the city-owned parking garages and lots in Baltimore City. PMS currently has 15 garages and parking lots under its management, and has created jobs for more than 70 employees. About 70 percent of her employees are Ethiopians; other employees come from diverse backgrounds. PMS Parking is also expanding, and has recently been awarded a major contract with a prospective partner, LAZ Parking. Together they will manage Metro Parks in Maryland, Virginia, and Washington, DC, which includes 49 parking garages in total. The new expansion will require about 100 employees, and will make PMS Parking one of the major players in the parking business in the tri-state area.

Overcoming Challenges

Five years after Amsale and her husband opened their first parking garage, in 1989, her husband passed away, leaving behind their son Mikael. They had been married for six years. Amsale had chosen to stay at home when her son was first born, but when her husband passed on she had to return to the business and manage it.

The future of the business was now in Amsale's hands. Her challenge was to take what had been built, which included five parking garages, and make it grow. It seemed that the weight of the world was on her shoulders. Her biggest challenge, she says was convincing her staff and clients that she had what it took to grow the company. Earning their trust was vital, and she had to work hard for it, she underscores.

Dealing with the competition was also a major challenge: They smelled blood when her husband died and she had to keep the sharks at bay. This required her to work up to 18 hours a day, and sometimes even longer to solidify her position.

Perhaps her biggest challenge, however, was how to take over the helm of the business while raising her son as a single parent. Balancing these objectives came at a price. She only saw his son on weekends, and even then she often had to take him into work with her. She returned home late at night often, just in time, she notes, to make sure that her son was sleeping restfully in his bed.

She recalls, "I didn't realize the effect that my continued absence from home had on my son until one day, I received a letter from his teacher imploring me to pay more attention to my son's needs." At the time, her son was six years old. He told his teacher that he was always left with a nanny because his mother was always at work. He also complained that she didn't play with him. Upon fully appreciating the situation, the teacher was moved to write Amsale a letter to beg her to spend more time with her son.

Amsale came to a stark revelation: On one hand she was making her business clients happy, but on the other, she was making her son unhappy. Realizing the toll the business was taking, Amsale decided to make some changes: She decided to balance her time between her business and her son. For the first time, she notes, "I started taking my son on vacations and spending quality time with him."

Reflecting on what was important to her, she said: "I wanted my son to be the best he can be and to grow up with the values I grew up with. To accomplish this, she realized she had be a more hands-on mother. She stepped up to the plate and changed her ways. She became more involved with her son and drew him into her world. She started showing him what she was doing at work and apprenticing him. She now wants him to work in different branches of her business so that he can gain exposure to the business world. She hopes that he will carry on her legacy in business but underscores that it is up to him to choose his career path in life. As for her part, she says that she will make sure that she has provided him with every opportunity to learn about business and to choose his own profession in the end.

Giving Back to the Community

In today's world, the lion's share of creating a balance in life is struck by reconciling work and home life. However, there is also a need to be a part of a community, Amsale notes. In her case, her community is broad: It includes Ethiopians, African-Americans, and the community at large.

As for her commitment to her Ethiopian community, she notes, "As an employer of many Ethiopians, I am doing my share to give back to my ethnic community.

But her commitment doesn't stop there. She is also concerned about the welfare of all Ethiopians in her community, whether they are her employees or not. She has been instrumental, for instance, in helping to build an active community center in Baltimore, which was started it in 1985.

The need for such a community resource became apparent to her when an Ethiopian refugee, who had come to Baltimore from Sudan, committed suicide because of depression. As she tells the story, "He had no family and couldn't speak English; the *Good Samaritan* charity organization had taken care of him for a while, but didn't know how to handle him. They had found him a job at a McDonald's restaurant, but he wouldn't take the job because he wanted a job as a gardener, which is the kind of work he had done back home. When he couldn't find the kind of work he wanted to do, he became so depressed that he stopped talking to anybody. An Ethiopian doctor was called in but to no avail, and in the end, he committed suicide."

"After hearing what had happened to him, my brother and others took the initiative to create an organization that would help Ethiopians, particularly newcomers, adjust to their new home," Amsale explains. She is now a major contributor to supporting the organization and its activities, which has doctors who provide health care assistance, and teachers who teach English to the new immigrants; it also helps new immigrants find jobs. She notes with pride, "We also recently opened a wing for an Ethiopian art collection at the Walter Arts Museum." She is also on the board of *Care Ethiopia*.

Amsale is also an active participant in Baltimore City After School Institute; Co-founder and board member of U.S. Care for Ethiopia Foundation; a board member of Ethiopian American Constituency; a member of the Maryland Lodging and Tourism Industry Association and of the African-American Chamber of Commerce; and a member of the Baltimore Downtown Partnership. She also believes in actively participating in the political process and engages in fundraising activities.

Dream On

Amsale still has time left to dream, despite her busy activities. She never stops dreaming about the future. Her next frontier is in real estate; since she has been working with empty parking lots for so long, it is only natural that she would start to think about building structures on the land. "My dream is to become a real estate developer," she says. In fact, it has been her dream for a long time. It is only natural to move in this direction; property development and garage expansion go hand-in-hand, she notes.

Amsale also dreams of helping her native country. Although she is aware of her responsibilities to her company, she hopes the day will come when she is able to go back home and open a training center that can help people to gain skills and to become productive citizens.

On the occasion of the 10th anniversary of her business in 1998, Amsale had the opportunity to reflect on her road to success. She shared the following remembrances with her friends, employees, and business associates:

"THANK YOU FOR OUR HOME"

I welcome each of you to the 10th anniversary celebration of our firm, the company with the memorable name. It is good to mark this milestone in the company of so many friends.

Good friends are always important in business. It is always the people around us who make the difference in our lives.

That is why I decided to invite my friends to the 10th Birthday Party of PMS Parking.

You are the reason I have my business.

You are the friends who have helped me to support my son, Mikael.

You are the reason we have a home in America.

For you to understand how important each of you is to me, I have to take you back before 1988, before there was a PMS Parking.

Getahun and I were young, then. We had left our homes in Ethiopia to get an education in America.

We traveled to a far-away place called Baltimore. We wanted to learn what America could teach us and take that knowledge back to Ethiopia.

We were young and carefree students, studying in a foreign land.
But while we learned about business and baseball,
while we studied history and ate crab cakes,
while we fell in love in a foreign land,
thieves came with guns in their hands
and stole our homeland.

So, I value you, the friends who have helped us create the business, which gives my son a home.

You gave us a home when our homeland was gone.

Getahun and I came to America carefree, the world changed
and we became refugees.

We had come to America to reach the stars,
and here we were, parking your cars.

But we worked hard, and we learned,
grateful to have a place that was safe,
to have work here in Baltimore, back in 1988.

And that is where you begin to enter our story, my Baltimore friends.

We decided to stay here, to become one of you, Americans, through and through.

We decided to take a chance on ourselves,
and a man named Elijah helped us to win
our first parking contract, the Holiday Inn.

Our business was started, but we needed to grow.
We looked to the City, but found the doors closed.
Just a few old firms, with friends in the know,
controlled all the work.
We had nowhere to go....

So we went to the Mayor.
We went to see Kurt,
and asked for some bids, to give us a chance -
He was fair, so he did.

The old firms decided
to give us a fight.
But Elijah stuck with us
and brought his friend, Mike.

When the bidding was opened,
when the fighting was done,
the old guard was broken,
and we had won.

That is the story of our beginning, friends. That is how two immigrants from
a tortured foreign land found a home in America.

The years that followed brought me the joy of our son, Mikael, and the pain of
losing Getahun.

In our ten years, we have known success and failure.

We have grown as a company. We now manage 2,500 parking spaces. We can
offer work to 60 people.

We still are not large, but we work hard, and we are growing.

You cannot know how grateful I am to all of you for being part of our American
story.

Unless you have been displaced from your home,
you cannot know what it is like to be alone
among strangers.

And that is why I am so grateful to all of you here.

To my friend, Mayor Kurt Schmoke, for giving us a chance.

To my friend, my former lawyer and now Congressman, Elijah Cummings,
for believing in us and turning our chance into a new start in our new country.

To my friend, Mike Christianson, for always being there when we needed
him.

To my friend, Herb Garten, for catching us when the world fell apart.
To my friend, Scott Phillips, for picking us up again.
To all of you, to all of the friends who have made America our home, Mickey
and I and all of rest of us at PMS Parking - the people who make our company
a family - say:

"Thank you, for taking us in."

"Thank you for giving us a home – and a new country."

We will never forget what you have done for us.

We will never, ever, let you down.

Lessons to Share

Amsale advises anyone who wants to start a business to be passionate about it and not to give in to naysayers. "I have been told many times that the parking services business was not for me. Even some of my family members thought that I might not be up to the challenge, given that I was a single mother. They tried to dissuade me from remaining in the business after my husband's untimely death."

"I understood their concerns, and, in some ways they were right, but I had a passion to carry on, and I am glad that I did. It is true that the parking business is male-dominated and that it was hard for me to stake a claim in the business as a woman, and to win the confidence of my employees and business associates, but I prevailed in the end. In fact, I am still the only black woman operating a parking business in Baltimore. Nevertheless, I remained strong and challenged my family and friends, and my commitment and steadfastness has landed me where I am today. I want to tell everyone, especially women: Don't let anyone tell you that you cannot do it."

Geta Asfaw
President
Ababa & Company, McDonald's Franchisee
Denver, Colorado

G eta Asfaw is an unqualified success, as an entrepreneur, and as an example of an immigrant who came to America and made it against all odds. He owns six McDonald's restaurants, employs four hundred workers, generates millions in revenue each year, and has won many awards for his contributions to his adopted Denver community. He also owns and operates a real estate and a securities investment firm. Perhaps the greatest measure of his success, he would say, however, is the fact that he has been able to devote time to his family and community while growing his business.

It is not entirely unexpected that Geta would emerge as an entrepreneur given that he grew up in the 1950s in the Merkato area, which is most vibrant market area of Addis Ababa, where he had an opportunity to see how business was conducted from the time he was a child.

The Merkato area, an open market in the western part of Addis Ababa, was created as a commercial center during a brief period of Italian occupation in Ethiopia in the 1900s. In the ensuing years, the Merkato became the largest open market in Ethiopia; all businesses are connected to it in one way or another. Without a doubt, the Merkato is Ethiopia's principal commercial hub and financial market; its ghetto-like and ramshackle structures and skyline of rusted corrugated tin belie its huge economic role: It has been estimated that over 60 percent of the country's money supply is within the Merkato's control at any given time. It has also been estimated that the average daily number of economically active people in the Merkato exceeds 150,000. Prices throughout the country are established in the Merkato through a web of business networks wholesalers, retailers, and brokers.

The awareness of and sensibilities to the marketplace formed Geta's early images of the business world. His observations drew him into that world and excited him. As he explains, "I think growing up in Merkato makes you smarter when it comes to business because you meet so many people from whom to learn."

Geta learned that one has to be tough to operate under Merkato conditions. His parents competed in the tough business world of the Merkato but they competed fairly. Geta notes, "As a child, I spent a great deal of time observing the deals in which they were engaged and learned a lot from my parents."

Despite the obvious significance of the role that the Merkato market plays in the Ethiopian economy, its entrepreneurs have not always been held in high esteem in the social order. The Gurages, however, are a special case. They have stood out for their entrepreneurial qualities and for their willingness to engage in manual labor, trade, and other money earning pursuits. Though their tenacity has often been met with prejudice, such attitudes only served to develop a strong sense of independence and networking among them.

Geta comes from a Gurage family on his mother's side. Though his father was not Gurage, his wife's family held him to Gurage standards in terms of making it in the business world. Geta explained, "Because of the strong entrepreneurial traditions of the Gurage culture, when my father proposed to marry my mother, her family was not happy because my father's family was not in the business field. You might say it was a bit of reverse discrimination."

He explains further, "In order to win my mother's family over, my father had to prove his business acumen. Fortunately, he was up to the task and, in fact, succeeded in business. In the process, my father instilled and inspired a love for business and business values in me that form the foundation of my beliefs today. One important lesson I learned from the way in which my father conducted business was that you must always value the customer and all with whom you interact in business. I also learned that there are learning opportunities to seize and build upon from every business encounter."

Lessons My Parents Taught Me

Geta learned from his father that you don't have to be born into an entrepreneurial family in order to succeed in business. "My father may have not come from an entrepreneurial family, but he was a born entrepreneur," Geta says. Explaining his father's background, he notes, "When he was just 13 years old, he started working as an apprentice mechanic. He was a quick learner, although he was illiterate. In a short time he was able to start his own business, a car repair shop. He soon branched out into other businesses as well, and started a taxi business. Next, he purchased heavy trucks, eighteen-wheelers, and before long, he had expanded into the bus transportation business. Geta's father, along with others, established a bus transport company as one of the first share companies (corporations) in Ethiopia.

Geta's father had a flair for marketing. He named his bus transportation firm *Wello Feres*. "Similar to the *Wells Fargo* company in America, my father's bus company played a critical role in opening up transportation routes that connected the provinces and major cities of Ethiopia."

One can see where Geta gets his business acumen. Noting his father's accomplishments in business, Geta explains, "My father's business grew so rapidly that he had to convert the heavy trucks he owned into buses in order to meet the demand for transporting people across the country. Ultimately, he had to import buses from Europe. Despite the growth of his transportation business, he continued to hone his skills as a mechanic, and in fact, served as the chief mechanic for the business. There was no mechanical problem that was too complex for him; he could fix any mechanical problem that arose with the buses, the eighteen-wheelers, taxicabs, and other vehicles."

There were many lessons Geta's father taught him. For instance, he learned the importance of setting goals from his father and about the importance of striving for excellence, he explained. Geta believes that many people are content to be average, but this is not the case for Geta. He says, "I don't strive to be average; I try to teach my children not to aim for mediocrity. I always tell them that when they think in average terms, they are going to be average, and their achievements and results will be average. I always compete with myself, and my goal is always to become a better person than I was yesterday."

Geta also learned a lot from his mother. As the saying goes, behind every successful man is a strong woman; Geta's mother was such a woman. According to Geta, his mother was an inspiration to his father and a major supporter of his business; though she didn't operate her own business, members of her family, including the women, operated businesses. Her mother, and her mother's sisters were the proprietresses of local bars, where they sold *Tej* (honey wine), Geta says. "To her, business was a good thing and she was proud of my father as a businessman."

Changing Times

Geta's parents, like many other parents of means, wanted to send their children to America to enable them to become doctors or lawyers, which, in their view, were the most prestigious professions. Geta shared his parent's dreams, and intended to become a doctor. He is quick to note, however, just because he wanted to become a doctor didn't mean that he didn't also want to run a business. He explained, "I wanted to combine my interest in becoming a doctor with my interest in owning a business, so I intended to own a clinic back home in Ethiopia."

Things got off to a good start for Geta when he was able to begin his university studies in America in 1972, but things would soon change. "I didn't know at the time that a dark cloud was looming over the political fate of Ethiopia, and that the dark cloud would ultimately cause a reversal in my family's fortune," Geta states.

In early 1974, Ethiopia entered a period of profound political, economic, and social upheaval. A confrontation between traditional and modern forces erupted and the entire political, economic, and social landscape was altered in the process. Soon after the Derg's rise to power, most commercial transport companies were nationalized, including Wello Feres. As a consequence, Geta's family was out of business and no longer in the position to support him financially, or to pay for his education. From that point onward, Geta had to make his own way.

On a Solid Academic Footing

It is just as well that Geta grew up in a hardworking entrepreneurial family because the time came for him to put his training to good use, now that he had to earn his own living in America.

When his financial position changed it became apparent that Geta would have to do things differently and to make new plans. When the political turmoil in Ethiopia erupted, he briefly returned to Ethiopia from America to check on his family's situation. His family gave him $1,000, which is all that they could spare. It would have to see him through until he could make other financial arrangements. His tuition alone cost $500 at San Francisco University, so he didn't have much left over to sustain himself.

As Geta said, "I knew I would have to work very hard to survive. My first decision was to transfer to another university in the U.S., to an area where the cost of living was lower. I was accepted at the University of Washington in Seattle, which I chose because I had a cousin, Ezra Teshome, who lived there and let me stay with him."

Geta would have to adjust his plan in other ways as well. He changed his major to political science in order to graduate earlier. Furthermore he figured, "Given what was happening in my country at the time, it seemed appropriate to study politics and international relations." He put his studies to use by becoming active in the Ethiopian Student Movement in the U.S., and focused on galvanizing support for democratic forces back home.

Geta never lost sight of his goal to graduate from the university, despite the changes in his plans. He graduated on time with a degree in International Relations, and with that victory under his belt, he continued on and obtained a Masters of Science in Political Science from the University of Washington. He finally felt satisfied that he had lived up to his parent's expectations.

Although armed with a number of academic degrees, he explained, "It was never my plan to work for someone else: I always knew I wanted to have my own business," Geta said. His degrees were obtained for the purpose of preparing him for the world of business, he explained.

He got his start in the work world by doing odd jobs. One of his jobs led to his current business in the food industry. "I worked in a restaurant as a waiter, for at least 45 hours a week, while also attending school. Although it was hard work, especially since I had to study at night, it was also a wonderful experience, because of where I worked, and because of the people with whom I interacted." Geta worked at *Heritage House*, which is an up-scale African-American restaurant in Seattle, where famous African-American entertainers such as BB King, Shaka Khan, the Blue Notes, and the Isley Brothers frequently entertained. Geta notes, "Because of the clientele they attracted, I was able to get generous tips. In fact, the tips were so good that I never needed to cash my monthly paychecks from the restaurant and this is how I first began to save money in America. "

Geta was always clear on his strategy and where he was going, and he never had any qualms about working his way from the bottom up. As he said, "I never thought I was too good to work in a restaurant, nor did I have reservations about taking on any other lower level job, for that matter. In fact, I took on many jobs to pay for my schooling, but working in restaurants was my favorite. I was not just a waiter, I became the head waiter and learned a lot about how to manage a restaurant." He adds, "I found that I loved the restaurant business, which was a rich training ground for me. It also gave me a chance to meet people from all walks of life, which in turn gave me a valuable insights into how people think, what services they like, and how they spend their money."

One of the biggest lessons Geta learned, he explained, was that if you love the job you are doing, you would do it well. Perhaps it was this lesson that made him place such a high premium on creating a positive working environment in his McDonald's restaurants, so that his employees would love their jobs, and do them well. In the process, he has gained their loyalty, which enables him to own twice the number of McDonald's restaurants of the average McDonald's franchisee.

A Partner For Life

One good thing began to lead to another for Geta. The best thing that happened to him was that he met his future wife. His positive attitude, his commitment to hard work, and his commitment to succeeding in life are among his traits that attracted his wife, who shares the same values. They met when they both worked at *Heritage House*. They were students at the time; she was studying at Central College in Seattle, while he was studying at the University of Washington.

Geta's wife, Janice Asfaw, is not Ethiopian; she is African-American. Their cross cultural union is very solid union and has helped to provide the foundation for Geta's success in business. Geta said, "We believe that we were meant for each other. We nurtured and developed our relationship for five years before having children, because we wanted to be sure that our union was solid and would last. Being so close to my own family, it was and still is unimaginable to me to ever consider the prospect of divorce, especially once we had children. We have been married for over 27 years now; the glue that keeps us together is love and mutual respect. We also share common political and social beliefs, and are business partners as well."

Life Before McDonald's

Before moving up the ladder to become a McDonald's franchisee in Denver, Geta worked in a 7-Eleven store in Seattle. After working in the store for a number of years, he got the chance to purchase his own 7-Eleven in 1979. As he stated, "You have to be ready to seize opportunities, and my wife and I were ready. We shared a commitment to saving money and because we both had had multiple jobs, we were able to save enough money to seize the opportunity to become business owners."

Geta has strong views about the importance of saving money. He says, "My wife and I agree that there is a difference between income and wealth: unless you can keep part of your income, you cannot build wealth, and from the very start, my wife and I always saved money. We never spent money unnecessarily; instead, we made wise investments. Even though we didn't earn a lot of income, the proportion of our income that we saved was very high."

Even now, Geta says, "We live below our means." For my wife and I, he explains, "it is not about impressing anyone with our clothes, cars, or other material things. Instead, we have always been focused on building our business." In his view, "it is not hard to make money in America; it is hard to save it. It is all about self-discipline and making short-term sacrifices." Geta remembers that some of my employees at 7-Eleven drove BMWs. One even had a Cadillac, while another one drove a Volvo. By contrast, Geta said, "I drove a small Toyota. In fact, many people used to think that I was one of the employees of the store, not the owner, because of the clothes I wore and the car I drove." His wife shares his values about how to live life, he notes.

External Financing

When asked if he ever obtained loans through the help of any government agencies, such as the U.S. Small Business Administration (SBA), Geta said that he had not. He also expressed dismay that many people think that all African-Americans require external financing to go into business when some in fact do have their own savings. It makes him a little angry when people assume that he had to access government financing to start his business. He didn't even know about such options, he explained, and when he learned about it, he opted not to access it because he didn't need it.

"It annoys me when people asked me if I received SBA loans or support to start up my businesses, or when people ask me if there is some kind of minority program through which I was able to get my stores, whether they are talking about the 7-Eleven or the McDonald's, Geta stated. He added, "When some people see African-Americans doing well, they have the perception that the only way that we are able to start a business is with a SBA loan, or through other sources of government support. What such questions suggest to me is that people don't think that African-Americans can succeed without such supports. While such supports are needed in some cases, there are also cases, such as ours, where we can compete on regular commercial terms," Geta stated.

Geta wants it to be clear that he is not saying that SBA loans and other supports that level the playing field are not important, because they are. But it is also true that there are many African-Americans who have made it on their own. With this caveat, Geta adds, "I encourage people to use whatever resources are available to help them start their business, including SBA loans. But you have to have some savings of your own, even to ask for SBA loans. When you have savings, it shows your commitment to the business that you want to start. SBA loans cannot be substituted for the savings you need to have in order to start your business; rather, they are intended to supplement what you have saved."

Developing People Skills: The Key to Success

The common thread in Geta's work experience is the need to communicate well with people. It is this experience that enables him to be an effective manager of his own employees. As he explains, "Running a 7-Eleven is an ultimate 'hands-on, people contact' business; if you can deal with the people and situations you encounter over a period of 11 years of running a 7-Eleven on a day-to-day basis, you are ready for any management challenge."

Geta has also learned about the importance of pleasing customers, motivating employees, and working with people of diverse backgrounds. As he states, "The key is that you have to treat people the way you want to be treated. I have many employees who have worked for me for several years, not because they could not get another job, but because they like the way they are treated."

"It is all about mutual respect," Geta adds. "In the end, I respect my employees and they respect me. When I go to one of my restaurants, I don't ask them to do things that I would not do. If I see that the floor or the restroom is dirty, I will clean it. When they see me doing that, what do they say to themselves? 'If the boss can do it, then it should be okay for me to do it.' I place a lot of stock in motivating my employees and demonstrating that there is no job I wouldn't do myself, no matter how small it appears to be."

Geta further suggests, "If you do not respect people, you will learn just how powerful even the smallest person in your organization can become. People can make you successful or they can hurt you. It doesn't matter what kind of job, level of income, or education they may have; they can hurt you if they want. A janitor, or even the person who parks your car, can either help you or hurt you."

"Oftentimes people pay closer attention and give respect only to people with political or financial power," Geta says. While this is appropriate, he underscores that the people who are going to make you successful are those who are working with you every day. "Those who cook the hamburgers, who work on night shifts and on holidays, and those who sweep the floors every day—these are the people who will help you succeed."

Going For the Gold—The Golden Arches

Geta had racked up a lot of experience by the time that he was offered an opportunity to become a McDonald's franchisee in Denver, Colorado. The one "snag" was that the offer was in Denver, and he was living in Seattle. To complicate matters, at the time, Denver was experiencing an economic recession and Geta says that many of his friends thought he was making a bad decision to leave all that he had built up in Seattle to move to an economically depressed area.

In Geta's view, however, while it was a big risk, it was not everyday that you get an opportunity to purchase a McDonald's franchise, so he and his family decided to take the risk and committed to the McDonald's training program. He undertook the training, which took two years, while remaining in Seattle. In the meantime, he and his wife continued to operate their 7-Eleven store.

Geta knows that many people think it is easy to become a McDonald's owner, but he knows better. As he states, "Becoming a McDonald's franchisee is no small feat; it is very competitive. There are about 15,000 applicants every year, and everyone who applies has the money to invest and the willingness to become a franchisee. Amazingly, however, out of an average of 15,000 applicants each year, McDonald's selects less than 100 people as new potential franchisees each year, Geta estimates. "Once selected for the program, applicants must commit to 20 hours a week of training, for at least two years." Surprisingly, even after completing the training program, the corporation retains the option of finally selecting you to be a franchisee," he underscores.

The McDonald's training program is very rigorous. According to Geta, it includes lessons on how to manage a McDonald's restaurant, on how to clean floors, how to serve customers, and on other facets of running a franchise. At each step of the way, you are evaluated on how well you take to all aspects of the training program, Geta explains. Only after you have completed the training program does the corporation render its decision about whether you have been selected for the franchise award. It is at this stage that you are also informed of where the franchise opportunity is available.

Once you get an offer, it is wise to take it, Geta states. Explaining how the process works, Geta notes, "If you are interested in a franchise at the location offered, you can negotiate a price. If you don't want to move to that area, you have to wait for the next round of offers. It can take some years before you get your choice of location. When I finished the training program, I was made the offer for a franchise in Denver, and I accepted."

Starting a New Life in Denver

It is difficult to be uprooted from one's home, but sometimes it is necessary. Geta and his family understood that and were ready to face the challenge of relocating. Geta drew strength from the lessons he had learned from his father's business experience, which demonstrated that when the going gets tough, the tough get going.

Geta remembers the hardship that his father had to go through when he lost his business, which was particularly heart wrenching because he had been one of the entrepreneurial pioneers in the country. Geta saw that despite the losses his father incurred, he was nevertheless able to adjust to a new set of circumstances and to chart a new direction for his life. Deep down, Geta felt that if his father could overcome such a devastating loss, the least he could do was to adjust to his new surroundings and take advantage of the business opportunity he was given.

There is no diminishing the human element associated with uprooting one's family. Accordingly, Geta had to think long and hard about his decision to move. He was particularly sensitive to his wife's attachment to Seattle, as she had grown up there and had long and deep roots in the community. However, in the end, they made a joint decision to take advantage of their new business opportunity and to move to Denver.

A Winning McDonald's Owner

Just because you have acquired a McDonald's restaurant, Geta quickly learned, doesn't mean that the road ahead is easy. In fact, Geta inherited a failing McDonald's restaurant, whose performance was on a steady decline. His challenge was to turn around the business, which meant winning over and maintaining customers, as well as attracting new ones. Given all of his previous training, he knew something about how to do this.

"My first task," Geta says, "was to 'shore up ship' and to develop a reliable sales team." His strategy for winning over his own staff was to treat them as he would have wanted to be treated. He never displayed anger or impatience and he let them know that while he expected them to take their jobs seriously, he also wanted them to have fun. "If the employees are happy it is contagious; customers will be happy, and they will come back again and again."

Geta believes that adhering to this philosophy has enabled every McDonald's restaurant he has taken over to increase its sales. For example, he said, "when I took over my first McDonald's, its sales had been going down for eight years; it downward slide was from $1.8 million dollars a year in gross revenue to $1.3 million dollars a year. In the first year after I took over the business, I increased its sales to $1.6 million dollars a year, and I have continued to expand sales ever since." Even when Geta operated his 7-Eleven stores, he increased its sales by 45 percent.

When asked what the key to his success has been, Geta replied, "Good people skills. Such skills create a win-win situation: the employees win, I win, and most importantly, the customer wins," says Geta. When the customer wins, you develop loyal customers and this is increasingly important in these competitive times. My philosophy is we don't just sell fries and hamburgers; we sell good service. You can get a hamburger from any place, but you will get the best service possible from our place of business."

Everything doesn't always go so smoothly, however. Geta notes. "It took me four years to acquire a second restaurant. After that, it was easier and now I have six. The biggest learning experience for Geta occurred in the process of expanding from one to two restaurants. As he noted, "I didn't have experience with running multiple businesses at the same time; operating in various locations and in different communities was quite challenging."

The next big leap and business growth spurt came in 1995 for Geta when he increased the number of restaurants he owned from two to three. This meant that he had to delegate tasks and responsibilities to a greater degree than ever before.

There were other challenges, too. For instance, he explained, "When I decided to acquire a third restaurant in 1996, the City of Denver refused to give me a building permit. Apparently, some of the neighborhood residents were not happy with the prospect of having a McDonald's restaurant in their neighborhood. It took us two and half years to fight the case, at considerable cost, but finally the city brought in mediators to settle the case and luckily I won."

Entrepreneurship and Franchising

People often wonder whether a franchise owner is really an entrepreneur. Geta, however, is clear on the fact that you must be both simultaneously. He explains, "If you are not an entrepreneur, the franchisor will not select you in the first place. What people don't understand is that many of the things created within a franchise comes from the owners. When we talk about franchisees, we are really talking about independent contractors. In our case, for instance, I don't work for McDonald's; when I owned a 7-Eleven store, I didn't work for 7-Eleven; I worked for myself."

Geta further clarifies, "In working as a franchisee, I pay royalties for the name and service fees in exchange for information about the market, the business format, and other pertinent matters. We use the franchisor as a resource to develop our business. However, as entrepreneurs it is up to us to make decisions that shape the future of our companies, and based on the decisions we make and the paths we follow, we either swim or sink." There is a lot at stake. Geta adds, "If you make the right decision you stay in business - if not, you are out of business. "

"Franchising has emerged as a means of standardizing various aspects of business management, but management alone cannot account for business success; a broader range of entrepreneurial decisions made by the franchisee ultimately determines success," according to Geta.

Geta further suggests that while the practical 'nuts and bolts' training on how to run your business is important, what is more important as a manager and entrepreneur is motivating your team. "I work with my employees to motivate them, and I give them examples of how to accomplish tasks. I also share my experiences with them so they can understand how to do a better job. This is not just in relation to the job at hand; sharing experiences in a broader sense encourages them to pursue their own dreams. Some of my employees who started out earning minimum wage now earn up to $60,000, without having gone to college, and this encourages others to strive."

The McFamily

Geta's business is a family business. It includes three of his sisters and a brother. One of his sisters, Tirsit, is responsible for operations of some of his franchises, while his other sister, Hirut, runs one of the restaurants. His sister Helen assists Hirut. "Tirsit has been with me since I owned my first 7-Eleven. She is very smart, and is good at what she does; she knows how the system works. She is the engine of our businesses." His brother Solomon is also on the fast track as a manager, and has also worked with Geta since he owned the 7-Eleven stores.

"My wife, Janice, and I also work together," Geta notes. "Anything I know about our business she knows, and anything she knows, she shares with me. We are a solid team. Even though I run the lion's share of the business, if something were to happen to me tomorrow, she could step right in and run the operation in a seamless transition."

"My wife has taken the training classes for both 7-Eleven and McDonald's, and has been approved as an owner-to-be. Our business has been a team effort from the beginning, and she is the Vice President of all the companies. At present, her day-to-day activities have been curtailed, as she is focusing more on raising our family and on giving back to the community as a volunteer, but if there is ever a need, she can step in and take my place."

The closeness of his family is not a surprise, nor is it an accident. As Geta explains, "My goal in life has never been just to succeed in business: I wanted to have a successful family. My parents have been married for over 50 years and are not just husband and wife; they are also friends. Similarly, my wife and I have been very close since we met first, and we have built our businesses together."

"Many people ask me how we have been able to work together and not have problems in our relationship; I tell them that it is not that we don't ever have any problems; we work them out. We stay focused on our goals, and are committed to one another. We respect each other, help each other, and share ideas. It really makes it easier when you have a partner and a spouse who can help and be an inspiration. We work as a team, and our relationship continues to blossom. I believe that it is more difficult for people without a family to achieve their goals; I attribute my success to our joint effort."

A Community Family

Geta is grateful for the opportunities he has had in America and is keen to give back to the community. He contributes to the National Association for the Advancement of Colored People (NAACP), the Urban League, and other community development institutions. He is also active as a McDonald's franchise owner, and draws on his training in political science. "When I came to Denver, the first thing I did was to create the Denver chapter of the National Black McDonald's Owners Association," said Geta. "I wanted to create a platform for business networking and for sharing business experiences and best-case practices among black owners. During my tenure, our advocacy also led to bringing more African-Americans into the system as franchisees and corporate employees. Similarly, I also was also the co-founder of the Black 7-Eleven Franchisee Association in Seattle."

Geta's interest in politics and societal development has not waned since starting his businesses. He is very much aware of the various forces in society, and has observed, for instance, that it continues to be a struggle for African-Americans to succeed. In his view, "As African-Americans, we have to work twice or even three times harder to achieve what others achieve in the business world. For this reason, I always look for opportunities to become involved with African-American organizations and self-help groups. For instance, I serve as a board member for the 'Hundred Black Men of America.'" He also serves on the Denver Chamber of Commerce and the Better Business Bureau, and works with the City Park of Denver and Denver Kids, just to mention a few of the organizations with which he is involved.

Geta also notes that when you help the community it helps you back. As he put it, "Business is not only about selling goods; it is also about selling ideas. Even though my goal when participating in community organizations is to help, it also helps me to understand the social and economic issues in my community, and provides an invaluable network of people that I can tap into at the same time." Geta also takes advantage of the political process in America and contributes to both parties. As a businessman, he believes that it is important to have some influence in both parties.

Many issues spotlighted in the political domain are not just 'pie-in-the-sky' issues for Geta. For instance, on the subject of diversity, Geta feels that it should not be just a slogan; it is a vital practice in his business. He is passionate about diversity and claims that embracing it is his top priority. As he states, "I work very hard to make sure that no one who works for me feels discriminated against in any way. Embracing diversity is not just a moral or social issue; it is also good for business, as people from different social and ethnic backgrounds bring their diverse experiences into our business."

Geta recalls, "I recently met a businessperson who told me that he did not believe in Affirmative Action. He said that he only cared about hiring the most qualified people for the job and that he had a test set up for his employees, and whoever passed the test, got the job. I disagreed with his view, arguing that it is not possible to administer a test that can predict how useful someone's diverse experience and background may prove to be in business. When we advocate diversity, it is not just to help African-Americans and other minorities; it is also to enrich our own experience and to improve the way we do business in our community." Geta practices what he preaches and notes that his promotion policy reflects his company's policy of diversity. He also notes that his policies also ensure gender diversity in his companies."

McAfrica?

You cannot help but wonder if Geta has thought about returning to his ancestral home to perhaps open a McDonald's restaurant one day, especially since Geta came from such a close-knit family. The McDonald's Corporation approached him in 1996 to consider opening a restaurant in South Africa. He and his wife were invited to visit the country, at the corporation's expense, and stayed for two weeks in Johannesburg. He said that while he seriously considered it, in the end, he passed on the deal.

Later, in February 2002, Geta notes, he was invited by Wellington Webb, former Mayor of Denver, and then-president of the National Conference of Black Mayors, and Chair of the International Committee of the U.S. Conference of Mayors, to participate in a business trip to Africa. He joined the delegation, and toured several countries in Sub-Saharan Africa. As a first generation immigrant from Africa, Geta commented on the difference between the business culture in the U.S. and Africa, noting, "When you are in America, there is always an expectation that you will meet a person, enter into business negotiations, and then close the deal right then and there. In Africa, by contrast, people take their time to negotiate and close a deal because they want to develop trust in you and to develop a relationship with you before they close a deal."

As to the viability of establishing a McDonald's restaurant in Africa, Geta points out that market size is the key factor. In many African countries, the purchasing power of the people is still low to be able to make a profit with such an investment at this time. Geta explains why it would be difficult to establish a McDonald's in Africa, noting, "The reality is that in America, the annual gross revenue of the average McDonald's restaurant is about $1.7 million dollars. The market size in a given African country would have to be large enough to match this sales volume. In addition, there are also other considerations. For instance, there needs to be a dependable supply chain, with quality products to supply our restaurants. In a nutshell, it is the economic growth and the market size in those countries that primarily determine whether or not a McDonald's restaurant would be feasible."

Nevertheless, Geta believes there are opportunities for Ethiopians in the Diaspora to invest back home. He underscores, however, that for this to

76

happen, Ethiopian expatriates have to be able to work with the political forces and institutions at all levels throughout the Ethiopian society. He adds, "The leadership in Ethiopia should realize that it is through entrepreneurial development that Ethiopia can find a path out of poverty. They have to listen to what investors are saying, in terms of policy and regulations, and they have to understand the power of entrepreneurship."

"Micro and small enterprises are the companies who pay the taxes and create jobs. They need to be supported," says Geta. He adds, "Until we have leaders who understand the power of entrepreneurs, it is going to take Ethiopia some time before we can see growth and development." Geta knows that the failure to recognize the importance of the private sector is not unique to Ethiopia. At the same time, he knows that everything cannot be expected to come from government; the private sector also has to play its role.

Geta notes, "The Ethiopian community in the U.S., for instance, is growing; I feel it is going to be a big force in the future. When our people return to Ethiopia as investors, they will not only inject financial resources into the country, they will also help in transferring new ideas and know-how. Therefore, politicians should place a priority on creating a positive enabling environment for investment for Africans in the Diaspora."

Advice to Emerging Entrepreneurs

Geta is clear about his goal in being an entrepreneur: It is to create wealth. He notes that in his case, he had such a desire; a desire not only to create wealth, but also to create a happy life. Geta underscores that creating wealth is important, noting, "A lot of times we can freely talk about politics, social issues, and other subjects, but not about money or about creating wealth. In my view, there is nothing wrong with building wealth; that is what business is all about. The reason why we get into business is not only to make money, but also to keep some of the money to build wealth."

"All over the world, if you look into every country, the people who build wealth, are the people who run the country," Geta says. "People who build wealth are the ones who share resources and the ones who pay taxes. There is nothing wrong with creating wealth, and there is nothing wrong with being rich, but you cannot create wealth if you don't save and take risks. Many people spend their time looking for guarantees and avoiding risks, which is a death sentence for success." Geta, however, notes that it is important to balance your goals in life because wealth alone does not bring happiness.

Before embarking on a business venture, Geta advises that it is important to reduce one's personal debts. Credit card debts, car loans, and other debts should be cleared, in his view, before starting a business. He says, "When people think about starting a business, they have to be very strong financially, and they have to sacrifice a lot. There are so many things we want to buy today. But, if you do that, you cannot create wealth. Once you build your wealth, then you can buy whatever you want, but you have to be prepared to make a sacrifice today."

Geta is a happy man and a wealthy man, but he does not measure his wealth in material possessions alone; he measures it in terms of his family life, his contributions to his community, and also in terms of his business success. He is still amazed by his success, and cannot believe it, as he said, "that a man like me, coming all the way from Ethiopia, could not only earn three college degrees, but has also employed over four hundred people, and owns and operates a multi-million dollar business—only in America, what a country."

Agonafer Shiferaw
President
Rasselas Jazz Club
San Francisco, California

B orn in 1952 and raised in Addis Ababa, Agonafer Shiferaw arrived in the United States in 1970 as a student. He studied management at San Francisco State University and landed a job with the local government, where he worked for 10 years. This was as he had planned; what he did not plan, however, was to become an entrepreneur. When entrepreneurial opportunity knocked, however, he answered. Today, although he is, as he calls himself, "an accidental entrepreneur," he is a very successful one, with twenty full time employees in his jazz club. As the owner of a jazz club on the famed Fillmore Street in San Francisco, he is not just in any business; he is in a business that is entwined with the heart of the quintessential American music scene.

It is perhaps surprising at first glance that an Ethiopian would become the owner of a jazz club in the heart of the jazz district in San Francisco. It is surprising because the connection between Ethiopians and jazz is not one that people usually make. But there is a connection. In fact, starting in the 1950s, Ethiopian musicians began to blend their music with jazz-fusions, demonstrating that Ethiopian music blends well with jazz because it sounds exotic to the western ear and its chords are commonly used in jazz.

Nevertheless, it is still surprising that an Ethiopian would be in the business of jazz and indeed in Agonafer's case, there is every reason to be surprised. There is nothing in his background that would have suggested that he would go into business, much less into the music business. It should be noted that in previous times, musicians in Ethiopia were not held in high esteem. Therefore, it would be unlikely that a person of Agonafer's relatively well-to-do social and economic position would aspire to be in the music world.

Agonafer was neither drawn to the business world nor to the music world when growing up. Rather, his dream was to work in the public sector. Even though his father and two of his brothers were in business, Agonafer had his sights firmly planted on joining the government. In order to prepare for his future, he like many other young aspiring Ethiopians at the time dreamed of becoming a professional and studying in America in preparation for his professional career. His brother followed this path and was already living and working in San Francisco. Agonafer's dream also seemed to be within reach.

Although Agonafer wanted to study in America, he planned on returning to Ethiopia. Part of his dream came true; he was able to study in America, but he wasn't able to return home. When the socialist Derg regime came into power in 1974, everything changed in Ethiopia and Agonafer's dreams of returning to the home he knew were shattered. The commercial farms that his father and brothers owned were nationalized, and Agonafer felt that he had no choice, under the circumstances, but to continue to reside in America.

He was lucky though: he landed a job with the City Administration of San Francisco, where he was first employed as a junior management officer. He worked with the city for ten years before he became an 'accidental entrepreneur.'

Agonafer reached a saturation point after working for the government for ten years and began to wonder whether he would be able to make his mark in society by continuing to work there. He made a bold decision to leave the security and comfort of his "9 to 5" job, and struck out on his own to start his own business. It is not a decision he pondered over for a long period of time; rather, it was one that unknowingly incubated within him. He didn't even know it was incubating in him until it sprouted forth.

As a student, Agonafer's social life was pretty much limited to the Ethiopian community. As he explained, "When I came to the U.S., I interacted mostly within the Ethiopian community and limited my direct contact with Americans. Almost all of my contact was with Ethiopians. One of the reasons I stayed so close to the Ethiopian community was because of the great political upheaval back home in Ethiopia; as overseas Ethiopians, we bonded together and engaged in robust political debates about what was best for our country." Working for the City Administration, however, gradually changed Agonafer's network and social circle. He noted, "I began to meet and know people of all of various backgrounds at my work place and eventually outside of work.

While Agonafer continued to expand his social network, he remained close to his Ethiopian compatriots. In the process, Agonafer came to know about the needs of his countrymen, and one of them was for a local restaurant that served familiar Ethiopian cuisine. At the time, there weren't any Ethiopian restaurants in the area, even though Ethiopians tended to be attached to their culture, cuisine and music. Agonafer spotted an opportunity: To establish a restaurant to cater to Ethiopians.

He didn't have a chance to seize this business opportunity right away, however. As he explained, "My first business was not a restaurant; it was a hardware store." This was because he could not access suitable premises for a restaurant. He explained further, "As I was looking for premises suitable for a restaurant, I came across a property in an upscale neighborhood, which I thought was ideal for a restaurant business. I discussed the matter with the landlord and learned that the space could be leased for a general hardware store, but not for a restaurant." He was disappointed but conducted market research of the area and became convinced that the location would indeed be ideal for a hardware store after all. Agonafer also recognized that he would have had to spend considerable time and resources to develop a market for an Ethiopian restaurant, so in the end, it made more sense to change his plans and open a hardware store instead of a restaurant.

"Using my own savings and some borrowed money from friends," Agonafer explained, "I was able to open a hardware store in 1984. Although I had no prior experience in running a hardware store, or any other business for that matter, I wasn't afraid: I knew that I could hire experts who would fill in the gaps of my knowledge and accelerate my learning curve. Most importantly, I believed in myself and knew I could be successful in any business if I committed myself to the endeavor."

A Hardware Store: A Hard Reality to Face

Agonafer had to face a number of difficult challenges as a new immigrant business owner in America. As he recalled, "One of the realities I was confronted with when I started my hardware store was the race issue. My hardware store was located in a primarily white area. As I was concerned about how this would play out for me, I decided to take matters into my own hands to diffuse the possibility of any negative, racially based opposition to me as the business owner. I hired a man of German descent, who had substantial experience in operating hardware stores, as the manager of the store." By hiring him, and putting him out front, Agonafer believed he could circumvent any racial prejudice that might affect his business.

Agonafer didn't let his ego get in the way: He instructed his manager to tell customers that he was the owner of the store, if anyone asked. Agonafer took this extraordinary step because, as he explained, as an immigrant, he wasn't sure how the customers would respond to him being the owner of the hardware store.

Dealing with the race issue was only one of his concerns. There were also other challenges associated with managing a hardware store business. The main one was that it is a relatively capital-intensive business. Agonafer explains, "Hardware stores typically have to carry between twenty and thirty thousand items, which costs a minimum of one hundred thousand dollars to set up. The carrying costs are high; although one has to carry significant inventory, demand is erratic. The point is, to be competitive; you have to have the goods in stock just in case someone might want it."

Creating a New Reality

When opportunity knocks, in order to hear it, you must be listening. Agonafer heard opportunity knocking loud and clear in 1986, when, after running his hardware business for two years, an opportunity emerged for him to lease a bar across the street from his store. The bar was located at California and Divisadero Streets, a few blocks away from the famous Fillmore Street.

It was time for a change and time to seize a new opportunity. Agonafer explained, "Although I had been running the hardware store successfully, and I was making money, I still wanted to open a restaurant. So, I leased the space in 1986 and started a restaurant business." He added, "There was a learning curve for me in this business because I had never worked in a restaurant before, but then again, I hadn't been involved in the hardware business either before I owned a hardware store." However, as Agonafer explains, "In any business the key is to be able to breakdown tasks and to solve them one by one."

In contrasting his experience in running a hardware store to running a restaurant, Agonafer notes, "In the restaurant business less inventory is required than in a hardware store business; the turnover is also higher in restaurants, and the profit margins are greater. In addition, the inventory costs in a restaurant business are a lot lower than in a hardware store business." Agonafer adds, "because the inventory costs are not usually more than twenty thousand dollars in a restaurant business, I don't have to tie up all of my money in inventory, so I prefer the restaurant business." In the end, Agonafer also learned that it is a great deal easier learning how to maintain clients for a restaurant than maintaining the inventory involved in a hardware store.

Not Just Any Restaurant...

There are restaurants and then there are restaurants. Agonafer did not just open any restaurant; what he did was bolder than that. He opened the *Rasselas Jazz Club*, a few blocks away from the famous Fillmore Street in San Francisco. To have a jazz club on Fillmore Street means something. Fillmore Street, after all, has an important place in American history, and in the history of modern jazz. It is where all of the leading jazz artists played during the mid-1960s, and part of its legacy was that it was part of the largest black neighborhood in San Francisco. In its heyday, the Fillmore District was heralded as the third largest commercial district in San Francisco. Famous jazz legends, including Duke Ellington, Count Basie, Miles Davis, Dizzie Gilespie, and Charlie Parker, performed on Fillmore Street. Its popular clubs included Jackson's Nook, The Plantation Club, the Booker T. Washington Hotel Lounge, Wally's Soulville, and Jimbo's Bop City, all of which were demolished in the mid-1960's by the San Francisco Redevelopment Agency as part of its neighborhood development project.

When the San Francisco Redevelopment Agency tore down the neighborhood in the mid-1960s; they ripped out the heart of the city. Fortunately, a renaissance began in the 1980s. With the renaissance, the seven blocks of Fillmore Street, between Sutter and Jackson Streets, soon became a Mecca for some of the city's most clever chefs, designers, and retailers.

The moment for the big move, from a few blocks away from Fillmore Street, to being on Fillmore Street proper came for Agonafer six years after he first opened his restaurant. In fact, it took Rasselas some years operating in a former location to build up its clientele and to position itself to be ready for the lights, cameras, and action of Fillmore Street. As Agonafer explains, "When I started my jazz club and restaurant in the mid-1980s, there weren't any jazz clubs operating in the area. I saw an opportunity to fill the gap and I seized it. I did not know much about jazz music at the start, but I learned."

The growth of Agonafer's restaurant business occurred when he introduced live entertainment. He gradually began introducing live entertainment to his restaurant, first with a piano player, then with a saxophone player, and finally with a vocalist. "The results were astounding. People started flocking in from all over, and before we knew it, we became one of the major jazz entertainment centers in the city," he explained.

The Business of Jazz

When asked if he plays jazz, Agonafer's answer is an unequivocal no. To the contrary, he explained that he felt a little uncomfortable, at first, with the notion of running a jazz club because he didn't know much about jazz. In the end, however, he came to the conclusion that although he may not have known about jazz music, he knew the business of jazz. Business is business, he believed, therefore it didn't matter if it was a hardware store or a jazz club, the same principles of running a profitable business applied.

Agonafer didn't realize it at first, but all the time he had served as a Senior Program Analyst in the local government actually came in handy; he had developed substantial analytical skills that he automatically drew on without even having to think about it. These skills enabled him to run two businesses simultaneously: he continued to own and manage his successful hardware store while also managing his jazz club.

Experience helps a lot, Agonafer notes. "It shortens the time it takes to learn the nature of business and allows one to put a business on a higher growth trajectory, faster. I started the jazz club without any prior knowledge of the jazz industry, so organizing jazz evenings felt more like on-the-job training. In fact, I sometimes felt that I might be embarrassed one day if someone were to ask me about the specifics of jazz music."

"Gradually, however, I figured out that there is a difference between the

Making It In America

business of jazz, and the art of jazz and what I needed to do was what I did best: Manage the business of jazz, rather than the art of jazz."

When musicians open a club, Agonafer explains, they sometimes fail because they are focusing on the music and not on the business. "By contrast, I think like a businessman and run my jazz club as a business, which does not imply that I lack concern about the quality of the product; I place a premium on quality.

Agonafer hastens to add, "The ability to balance the quality of the product and bottom-line income you generate, comes through experience. Although I am not an expert in financial management, by looking into how things work, I am able to tell which services are making money and which ones are not." Agonafer also noted, "I have a sense of conceptualizing organizations, and a good grasp of how organizations work, be it public or private. My role as the owner and manager has been to identify an opportunity, to organize it into a business, to structure the business in a manageable way, to assign the tasks, and then to manage it. I believe these qualities have helped me overcome whatever shortcomings I had in terms of hands-on experience and my bottom-line figures confirm that we are managing the business in a sustainable manner."

Getting in the Business Groove

Rasselas Jazz Club and Restaurant has taken off and is an unqualified success. As a growing number of clients from varied backgrounds began to patronize the club, it became clear to Agonafer that he would have to get more into the 'groove of the music' to understand what his customers were most interested in, and to determine how to stay ahead of the competition. So, he began to travel to other cities outside of the Bay area to see how other clubs organized live entertainment events and to check out different musicians. Before long, he was in the jazz groove and knew who was who and what was what in the industry.

Agonafer is "into" his business and wants to see it grow; not surprisingly therefore, he is constantly trying new things. For instance, he invited the rising San Francisco based bandleader, drummer and percussionist Babatunde Lea to play at his club. He also invited piano legend Hilton Ruiz, saxophone phenomenon Ernie Watts, and bassist Geoff Brennan to play together for four nights of jazz steeped in the rhythm of the African Diaspora.

Rasselas Jazz Club also co-sponsored a series of concerts with Babatunde's new label, Motema Music, and with the "Edu-cultural Foundation," a non-profit organization that teaches critical thinking about social and cultural issues through the arts. The concerts mark the first of a series of cutting-edge jazz residencies that are taking place at Rasselas on Fillmore Street. By offering San Francisco audiences a new venue to hear innovative jazz in an intimate concert setting, Rasselas joins the growing Fillmore Jazz preservation movement to solidify San Francisco's legacy as a vibrant jazz scene.

There is always another mountain to climb in business. For Agonafer, it was owning the property where his club was located. Given the growing popularity of his club, he didn't want to lose his lease, so it was important to be able to purchase the real estate. Fortunately for him, the owners were willing to sell it to him. Up to this point, he had been running the hardware store and the jazz club simultaneously, so when the opportunity presented itself to be able to purchase the real estate where his club was operating, he seized the opportunity and decided to sell his hardware store in order to use the proceeds from the sale to purchase the jazz club property.

Behind the Big Move to Fillmore Street

There is a lot of skill involved in Agonafer's rise in business; there is a lot of luck as well. Arguably, had Agonafer not worked in the city government, he may have not been approached by the city to be one of the anchor developers in the Fillmore District revitalization project.

Agonafer was given an opportunity by the city to bid on space within the city's new revitalized Fillmore Street building project. In the mid-90s, the same agency, the San Francisco Redevelopment that had torn down the neighborhood wanted to revitalize it. The agency also decided to use jazz as a marketing tool for the revitalization of the area. The aim was to create an atmosphere similar to New Orleans' French Quarter Jazz District. The City Council issued a Request for Proposal (RFP) throughout the nation, inviting small businesses to bid on the premier location. Two firms won: the Blue Note Club from New York, and Rasselas Jazz Club, from San Francisco.

With the help of a sizeable loan from the city's Redevelopment Agency, Agonafer invested more than $1 million to transform the location, at 1534 Fillmore Street, from the neighborhood of an existing meat and fish market, into an elegant lounge, nightclub, and restaurant with more than 6,000 square feet. In 2000, Rasselas finally moved into the Fillmore Street bringing back live jazz where it belonged.

When he first started Rasselas, he took out a five-year lease, with an option to buy the building. He told the press, "It will take a lot of time, but we're going to be here for a long time...I take this as a big responsibility to be a part of this community, and I promise to maintain the delicate balance between sensitivity to the artists and a solid understanding of the business side of jazz."

As a businessman, Agonafer always knew that he would have to face competition, especially if he succeeded with the club, and he was prepared for that. He knew, for instance, that the famed Blue Note Club would soon arrive on Fillmore Street. The view he expressed about his competitor is: "The Blue Note is a different caliber of nightclub, with more than 10,000 square feet of space and international financing so they can afford to book international talents." By contrast, he concentrates on national and regional talent and notes, "we'll complement each other."

While the revitalization project has been slowed, Rasselas Jazz Club is now firmly grounded at Fillmore Street.

Beyond the Music

Agonafer is always on the move. Never one to let the grass grow under his feet, by the early 1990s, he began to make investments in real estate and now owns apartments in Oakland and San Francisco. He notes that it has not always been a smooth ride, explaining, "When I first started investing in real estate in 1989, I bought at the top end of the market. Thereafter, when the economy entered into recession in the early 1990's, property values plummeted and I was wiped out. I had to go through various financing modalities, including taking secondary mortgages to stay afloat in the business. But in another way, I was lucky: I knew people who could support me. I made a mistake and didn't consult people who knew the business when I bought the properties because I thought I knew it all. In reality, there were things that I could have done better if I had sought out professional advice. "

Agonafer has learned from his mistakes. He says, "I have learned that assuming you know everything can put you in a difficult position and cause irreparable damage to your business. When you are confronted with business options and you don't know which direction to take, it is important to consult with professionals and to get proper legal and professional advice rather than relying on your own gut feelings. My advice to others is to go out there and share your issues with someone who can advise you on them."

Agonafer has also learned a lot about the importance of building social capital. In fact, he explains, "One of the biggest lessons I have learned is that you must build and draw on social capital to succeed in business. My Ethiopian compatriots helped me stay afloat during difficult times, and some of my friends even acted as cosigners of my loans when I first started out in business. This does not mean that I solely relied on the Ethiopian market or clientele. To the contrary, I worked hard on customer handling to attract a non-Ethiopian customer base. We also marketed to everyone, not just to Ethiopians. Our goal was to bring customers back once they visited our club. Today, Asians, Whites, and others all feel comfortable spending time at the club today."

Based on his own positive experience, Agonafer believes that Ethiopians living in America have great potential to grow in entrepreneurship. He also feels this is an opportune time, as America is embracing diversity, for Ethiopians to take advantage of their growing presence in America and their cultural and psychological strength.

It is a good time for Ethiopians to forge deeper and greater alliances with African-Americans and to take advantage of the business support systems and government resources that are available for minorities, Agonafer says. He also says, "Ethiopians have to learn to take advantage of these opportunities. We need to conceive of new business forms as well, not just to imitate existing businesses. Ethiopians have a particularly important asset for business, which is discipline and hard work. Nevertheless, many of us are not getting the right business advice, and as a community, we lack strong organizations that facilitate networking." Agonafer believes that many Ethiopians underestimate their capacity for business and fail to take advantage of their potential.

Motivation and Inspiration

Although money is a motivating factor in business, Agonafer knows that a sole focus on making profit does not make for a happy life. As his experience shows, "Once you achieve a certain financial return on your investment and a certain comfort level, accumulating additional wealth ceases being a motivating factor. The fun is in the idea of creating a business. I don't think people open chains of businesses from one location to another just because they want more money. It is the desire to create something and to succeed in what they do that motivates them, and I think that is what capitalism is all about: It is not so much about making money or about the profit margin; it is about seizing an opportunity and making something happen. The challenge of how far you can go with your ideas, and the thrill of making it happen, becomes more important as a motivating factor."

"The desire to create a legacy is also an important motivating factor, as is the desire to be the best you can be. External competition does not motivate Agonafer; internal competition does.

Investing Back in Ethiopia

Agonafer has not forgotten about his home country. He says, "I have been to Ethiopia a few times; I have seen a lot of new activities there and some positive developments. One area of investment that is very attractive is real estate." According to him, there is a lot of potential to realize great returns on real estate investment in Ethiopia. At the same time, Agonafer sees the need for expanding the role of private sector in the economy. He notes, "In Addis Ababa, for instance, you see a small property that costs millions of Birr standing next to a big plot of land with nothing on it, and you ask who owns it and they tell you that it is government property." It is clear, Agonafer states, "that the government needs to let go of its hold on property and open it up to the private sector for ownership." He also underscores, "In the final analysis, you can't execute capitalism halfway."

Agonafer also believes that Ethiopians in Diaspora have important role to play in bringing needed capital and technology to Ethiopia. In contrasting the decision making of non-Ethiopian foreign investors to Ethiopian foreign investors, Agonafer notes, "While the former may take a number of economic and political factors into consideration, for Ethiopians, investing in Ethiopia has intrinsic value beyond financial returns."

Dr. Teame Embaye
President
Nile Chiropractic, Inc.
Minnesota

orn in 1963 in Fatsi, a small town in Tigray, northern Ethiopia, Dr. Teame Embaye has come a long to America to make his dreams come true and to be in a position to dream otherwise unimaginable dreams. Brought up in a strong entrepreneurial family, Teame knew something about business but he knew little about different professions, and he knew nothing about the field of chiropractic medicine. He closed his knowledge gap in America years later and eventually opened his own chiropractic clinic in St. Paul, Minnesota in 1997, and some years later another one in Minneapolis.

The roots of chiropractic care, it turns out, can be traced back to the beginning of recorded time. Writings from China and Greece dating back to 2700 B.C. and 1500 B.C. mention spinal manipulation and the maneuvering of the lower extremities to ease lower back pain. Hippocrates, the Greek physician who lived from 460 to 357 B.C., also published texts detailing the importance of chiropractic care. In one of his writings he declares, "Get knowledge of the spine, for this is the requisite for many diseases."

Dr. Thompson, a Canadian, who was sent to Ethiopia after the end of World War II by the Allied High Command to help rebuild the country after it was liberated from the fascist occupation, introduced chiropractic medicine to

Ethiopia in the 1950s. He opened a large clinic to treat lepers and also treated patients with chiropractic techniques, with the assistance of his wife Hazel, who was also a doctor specializing in chiropractic medicine. They trained students in chiropractic techniques and two of their students later trained at the first chiropractic college in America, the Palmer School in Iowa, and became Ethiopia's and Africa's first doctors of chiropractic medicine. Teame was not aware of their accomplishments when he was growing up, however.

Clearly, there is a great need for chiropractic doctors in Ethiopia, as many people earn their living by doing manual work, toiling for long hours in the field. If only they could have access to chiropractic services their burdens may have felt a little lighter.

Teame was lucky: he did not have to labor in the fields when he was growing up. In the small town of Fatsi, his parents owned and operated a merchandise store and a hotel. His father also traded livestock between Tigray and Asmara when Eritrea was part of Ethiopia. By observing his father, Teame gained a positive impression of the business world and felt that entrepreneurship was an honorable profession.

Teame was involved in the various family businesses. When he wasn't in school, he helped his parents by working at their restaurant as a waiter as a cashier and as a procurer of vegetables. In the process, Teame learned many lessons that would come in handy later when he established his own medical practice. Two key lessons he learned were the value of hard work, and the importance of ethics in business and in life.

Most importantly, his parents served as role models and as examples of the importance of being earnest, persistent, and determined in business. However, the family's good times came to an abrupt halt, as they did for so many other Ethiopians, when the civil war of the 1980s in northern Ethiopia led to the closure of their businesses.

One Picture is Worth a Thousand Words

Teame's first professional goal was to become an agricultural services expert because he observed the work such experts did in the field and found meaning in it. To pursue his goal, he attended the Jimma Agricultural College from which he earned a two-year diploma. As he had hoped, he was hired by the Ministry of Agriculture upon graduation, and was assigned to Asmara, where he worked for the next four years.

What was exciting about being an agriculture extension officer, according to Teame, was the opportunity it afforded to travel—even if it was only to the suburbs and to rural areas. Riding on motor bicycles and having a chance to meet new people was fun; he also taught farmers how to improve their agricultural and animal husbandry techniques. In a typical day's work, Teame went from one village to the next to inspect and demonstrate vegetable and cereal plantings. He demonstrated the benefits of applying modern techniques and fertilizers and showed the farmers how to use improved seeds.

The fun did not last, however; the bubble burst when he realized that the extension programs were under-funded and that the actual demonstrations were few and far between. Teame was also disappointed that his work was confined to the suburbs of Asmara because of the ongoing civil war at the time.

One of the good things that came out of his work in the area was that he met an Indian doctor in Asmara who was working for the government hospital and who also had a private clinic. He developed a friendship with the doctor and as their friendship grew, he often visited the doctor at his clinic where he was able to observe him helping patients. He took note of the fact that most of clinic's patients were in higher income brackets and could therefore afford private care. He also noted that although the Indian doctor worked long hours, he seemed to really enjoy what he was doing. He also observed that the doctor made good money, more than any agricultural extension expert would ever make. Before long, Teame had a new dream: to become a medical doctor.

How to Get From A to B to "Be"

When Teame decided to study medicine he joined scores of other Ethiopian dreamers who dreamt of going to America to study medicine. However, he was quickly confronted with the reality that there weren't any scholarship opportunities to facilitate his studies in America. Instead, like others in Ethiopia at the time, he was offered a scholarship in 1984 to attend university in Bulgaria in Eastern Europe. He jumped at the chance, even though it was to study agriculture rather than medicine.

He studied agriculture for one year until switching his major to medicine. In 1985, after completing his first semester of studying medicine, he took a vacation in Romania. Once there, he kept going—to Poland, then to East

Germany, and then to West Berlin, where he applied for refugee status. His ultimate goal was to get to America, he explained. "In order to get to the U.S., I had to go through a number of countries because people who resided in Bulgaria were not allowed to enter Western countries; the only way I could get out from Bulgaria therefore, was to go through all these countries in order to enter West Berlin," Teame said.

Teame added, "Once in West Berlin, I applied for refugee status at the U.S. Embassy." The process entailed being interviewed in West Berlin, then being transferred to West Germany to wait while my application was processed." It took about eight months, Teame explained, until he was finally admitted as a refugee to the United States in November 1986. Upon being granted refugee status, he immediately moved to New York; and one month later, he moved to Minneapolis, where he had a cousin who was attending graduate school. "My cousin, Gebru Gayeem, showed me the ropes and gave me the foundation I needed to pursue my dreams in America," Teame said.

Poetic Justice

The only work he could find when he first moved to Minneapolis was that of a janitor. He mused, "Perhaps it was fitting that I had to do back-breaking work as a janitor on my road to becoming a chiropractor so I could appreciate the need for chiropractic care."

Indeed, the hard work he performed gave him a new found respect for why the field of chiropractic medicine is needed: To help those who engaged in back breaking work. In fact, Teame noted that he worked so hard as a janitor that he needed chiropractic care himself. But he didn't complain about being a janitor; it was the only work he could find and he was happy to have a job. Interestingly, the first patient of Daniel Palmer, the father of Chiropractic field, was a janitor who worked in his office.

While working as a janitor, Teame kept his goals in sight; finally, the State University of Minneapolis accepted him for admission, and gave him a new job as a research assistant. He noted, "Although my salary did not go far in terms of paying for my education, at least it was something."

Teame remembers, "Life as a student was harder than I expected. The work was intense and I didn't have time to make friends; in fact, I had no time for anything but studying." Upon reflection, he believes that his fellow students thought he was 'stuck up' because he didn't socialize with them. In fact, all he had time for was studying; though he now wishes he had made the time to get to know his fellow students better.

Teame faced many challenges at university and one of them was being the only minority in his class. It wasn't just being a minority that was difficult; the difficulty was as a minority, he had fewer resources than his classmates. As he recalled, "Many of my classmates came from wealthy families and seemed to know what they were going to do after they graduated." Contrasting their situation with his, he noted further, "Most of them had the means to buy their own clinics, or if not, they could work with their parents. In my case, however, I didn't have a family who could provide me with financial support to start my own clinic. At the time, I also felt that I didn't have a social network to tap into to get a job, and even if I could manage to open a clinic, it was overwhelming to think about the challenge of getting clients."

Not only was Teame a minority; he was also an immigrant, which had its own set of challenges. As he put it: "As an immigrant and a minority, the odds seemed to be stacked against me. Sometimes it seemed as though all of my hard work would be in vain. When the odds seemed insurmountable, I thought of my parents for inspiration and remembered never to give up: perseverance is key. After eight years of school, I finally graduated in 1996, with both my undergraduate and graduate degrees."

There were a few bumps in the road for Teame as he navigated his way through school and the social system in America, but none of the problems he encountered were insurmountable. As he explained how he dealt with the problem of racism and discrimination in particular, he noted: "I became aware of and experienced subtle forms of discrimination at various points, both while I was studying and after I graduated. For instance, it manifested itself in professional networks, in insurance companies, and in the competition. I resolved, however, that life is full of challenges, and that racism and discrimination are just some of the many challenges one has to overcome." He added, "Whenever I experience discrimination or racism, I challenge it in the appropriate way, either through legal means or through direct communication. I am not discouraged easily and I have never been dissuaded from pursuing my dreams, even when it seemed that the odds were stacked against me."

Alternative Medicine: An Alternative Life

In commenting on his choice of profession, Teame is very clear about the special contribution that chiropractic medicine makes. He explains the field, noting: "Chiropractic medicine is sometimes referred to as alternative medicine. It combines biomechanics and neurology, and focuses on muscular and skeletal disorders of the body; it is also concerned with and promotes the human body's ability to heal itself without the use of surgery or medication. The field is also relatively new, and although I never planned to study this form of medicine, I am glad that I chose it because there is a lot of room for future innovations in the field. My particular specialty is biomechanics, focusing on the structure and function of the spine. Specifically, I focus on the biomechanics, structure, and function of the spine and its effects on musculoskeletal and neurological systems in the preservation and restoration of health."

It has taken some time to build the profession in America, but slowly in the twentieth century, doctors of chiropractic have begun to gain legal recognition. A continuing recognition and respect for the chiropractic profession in the United States has led to growing support for chiropractic care all over the world, in turn. The research on chiropractic care that has emerged from around the world has also yielded influential results, which have changed, shaped, and molded perceptions of chiropractic care everywhere.

Various studies have suggested that chiropractic care has the potential to save hundreds of millions of dollars annually by preventing disability payments and improving health. Furthermore, doctors of chiropractic have become pioneers in the field of non-invasive care, promoting science-based approaches to a variety of ailments. There is a growing consensus that dedication to chiropractic research could lead to even more discoveries in preventing and combating maladies in future years, and this is what draws Teame to the practice, he explains.

The Practice

Teame was lucky: After graduating, he landed a really good job in a multidisciplinary clinic that enabled him to develop his skills and expertise, and to get his first glimpse of how a clinic operates as a business. Teame worked for a practice that consisted of three medical doctors, two chiropractic doctors, and a number of physical therapists. Everything ran smoothly in the clinic and Teame soon began to imagine that he too could have a clinic. His confidence was boosted when clients started requesting him by name.

Teame had only worked as an employee for ten months before he struck out on his own and opened his own clinic. He had done well in his previous employment, so much so that he was honored as the clinic's doctor of the year, and was given a week's vacation in the Bahamas. Upon reflection, he noted, "This became a turning point in my career; I decided to become an entrepreneur. Ever since I dreamed of becoming a doctor, I have always wanted to run my own clinic; it was the goal that I traveled all the way from Ethiopia to pursue. Now the time arrived, so I quit my job to start my own clinic in St. Paul, Minnesota."

His belief that he could succeed with his own clinic proved to be correct. His first clients came to him through his connection with his previous employer but thereafter he attracted clients through referrals and word-of-mouth as his reputation grew.

It wasn't all smooth sailing for Teame, however; he, like many others, had to pay his dues and go through growing pains when he started his business. He recalls, "Starting my own clinic was not easy. For the first six months I was making less than half the money that I had made as an employee; on top of that, I had to work longer hours, take care of administrative and financial matters, and build a customer base. I was also at a disadvantage because I did not have a developed social network that could support me and worse yet, I didn't have anyone with whom to share my experiences."

Sometimes it's lonely for entrepreneurs when they first start out and this was the case for Teame. As he tells it, "It was just me, myself, and I, and I could not afford to fail." In Teame's case, failure was not an option. Luckily, things worked out for Teame's business. Within a year, he says, he was able to create a loyal customer base and to transform his clinic into a viable business venture.

Teame became so successful that he was soon able to open another chiropractic clinic in Minneapolis. He now has four doctors and one assistant working in his two clinics. He also plans to open chiropractic clinics in Washington, DC, Maryland, and in Virginia, where there is a large Ethiopian community."

It Takes a Village

The key to having a successful clinic is having customers; Teame knew this. So, he put a lot of effort is undertaking the necessary research to identify target clients. As he explained, "I wanted to start by targeting the underserved market of East African immigrants, including Ethiopians, Eritreans, and Somalis, in Minneapolis and St. Paul. The problem I found was not figuring out whom to target, but rather how to raise the capital I needed to launch the business. The equipment is expensive, the overhead is high, and you need reserves for unforeseen financial needs."

Before he opened his first clinic, Teame had promises from friends to provide the financing needed. When he quit his job to start his own clinic, however, Teame was disappointed, finding that most of those who promised to come to his rescue did not come through. "Only one person, Mesele Abraha of Denver, actually delivered on his promise," said Teame.

Teame looked on the bright side, however and noted, "Even though most of the people who said that they would invest didn't do so; they still encouraged me, and I am thankful for that." He did have to adjust his course, however. He explained, "When my friends let me down, I didn't know where to turn. I wasn't aware of various government supported loan programs, such as the Small Business Administration's guaranteed loans, at the time. Therefore, instead of buying a clinic, which was my original idea, I had to sublease my premises, and work for a year before I was able to buy my own clinic."

Healing a Community

While some might overlook potential African clients, Teame doesn't. He knows that Africans need chiropractic care too. Until recently, he notes, "he was the only African doctor servicing the Eastern-African community in the Minneapolis, St. Paul area. His comparative advantage, he says, is that many people of diverse backgrounds feel comfortable coming to see him; they feel that he understands them and their needs because he understands their culture better and can communicate with them easily. He also speaks a number of languages: Amharic, Tigrinya, English, Spanish, and Bulgarian, which help him reach a wider community.

Teame is excited about the chiropractic profession and about the prospects of encouraging young people to think about careers in the discipline. But he adds, "In addition to promoting the supply of chiropractors; it is important to promote demand for the service, especially among immigrants who are not as familiar with the discipline. My colleagues and I therefore try to educate our community. We provide health screening, diagnose the elderly, and provide other services for free in order to showcase the benefits of chiropractic care."

Teame adds, "Those who practice chiropractic medicine cannot spread the word alone: we need a wide network of friends and professional associates in various fields that can also espouse the benefits of chiropractic care." This point reminds him of the fact that when he was at university, he didn't spend enough time on network and relationship building. Now, he sees just how important such relationships are and how professionals in different fields have to cooperate.

Teame also thinks about the prospects of promoting chiropractic medicine back home in Ethiopia. He explains that introducing chiropractic medicine, as part of the health care system in Ethiopia is not a small task; it requires the reorganization and reorientation of existing academic and health institutions. Because chiropractic care can treat various illnesses such as skeletal disorders, asthma, headaches, arthritis, and other ailments and has the potential to save financial resources that are currently being diverted to western medicine, it is worth introducing it into the system. There are studies that show that chiropractic care saves more than $13 billion dollars a year from cancelled surgeries, and with this potential to save money, Teame strongly believes that more emphasis should be placed on promoting the field in Africa.

Married to the Job

Teame has had to make some trade-offs to succeed. One thing he traded off was his private life. He explains, "So far, I have put all of my energy into developing my practice, but it is now time to put more energy into building my life." He adds, "I am single, but hopefully I will marry before long. Now that I am making more contacts in the community, I believe that I will be able to meet someone with whom I can share my life and my future dreams."

Teame also has future goals in his profession. He notes, "There is still so much I want to do in my field. I don't want to be a clinician for the rest of my life; my future goal is to work as a researcher in alternative medicine.

Currently, I am earning a masters degree in Healthcare and Human Service Administration, and as I continue to study, my hope is that I'll be able to work with a research-oriented institution, such as the National Institute of Health (NIH), or the Red Cross in Africa."

Lessons Learned

Teame advises emerging entrepreneurs to have a goal that inspires them, to which they can commit themselves. He explains, "It's not that you can't modify your goals from time to time, but whatever your goal is, you have to work hard to overcome the obstacles associated with achieving it." As he observed from his parents, and now knows from firsthand experience, "The key to achieving goals is hard work, persistence, and discipline. Nothing comes easily: you must persist until the goal is achieved."

Teame adds, "America is a land of opportunity, where you can make your dreams come true; there are all kinds of opportunities that people can take advantage of here. You can attain your goals and realize your dreams here; young entrepreneurs must take advantage of these opportunities."

On how to start a business, Teame advises, "It is important to save as much money as possible because nothing replaces savings. However, there are many sources that people can tap into for financing these days, sources that I didn't know about when I started my business. Anyone who wants to start a business should find out about sources of financing and access them if needed." The key, Teame explains, is to use every resource available.

Another important lesson he has learned, that he passes on to the next generation, is: "Never be too busy to build your network in your own community. One day, it may be your salvation."

Adem Araro
President
Stop 4 All Food Mart
Washington, DC and Maryland

Born in 1954 in Dodola, a small town in the Bale province of Ethiopia, Adem Araro grew up between Dodola and Dilla, in Sidamo, which is the main coffee growing area of Ethiopia. His family, like many others in the area, was involved in the coffee business, but as traders rather than as growers.

The story of coffee has its beginnings in Ethiopia, the original home of coffee Arabica, which still grows wild in the forest of the highlands. Legend has it that Kaldi, a goat herder from Caffa, Ethiopia, first noticed the effect of coffee beans on the behavior of his goats. He noticed that his goats became hyperactive after eating the red "cherries" from a certain plant, when they changed pastures. He tried a few himself, and soon became as overactive as his herd. According to legend, a monk happened by and scolded him for "partaking of the devil's fruit." However, the monks soon discovered that this fruit from the shiny green plant could help them stay awake for their prayers.

It is alleged that there are Arabic scientific documents dating from around 900 AD, which refer to a beverage drunk in Ethiopia know as 'Buna' (the word for coffee), and which confirm that coffee was first grown in Ethiopia.

According to these documents, the Mufti of Aden visited Ethiopia in 1454 and saw his countrymen drink coffee there. He was reportedly impressed with the drink that cured him of some affliction, and his approval made it soon popular among the dervish of Yemen, who used it in religious ceremonies, and introduced it to Mecca.

Coffee has long been Ethiopia's most important cash crop and export commodity. Ethiopia produces and exports arabica beans, the best quality coffee of the world, and some 12 million people are dependent on Ethiopia's coffee industry. The Oromo or Worji group, to which Adem belongs, has possessed knowledge of the coffee business for generations, going back to the days when such trade necessitated forming strategic alliances with Arab traders.

The coffee business is not without intrigue and a lot of vested interests. Therefore, to be successful in the coffee business, one needs to be very skillful. Adem's family members were indeed very skillful in business and possess the high level of skill that is required to negotiate with local farmers to purchase the coffee, and to resale it in the domestic and foreign markets through an extended network of local and foreign traders.

According to Adem, practically everyone he knew when he was growing up was involved in the coffee industry, in one way or another. The same holds true for his wife's family. Adem, in fact, was the only salaried worker in his family, he says. As he observed the business as a child, he understood that it was a commodity-based business, and that when the price of the commodity plummets, so do family fortunes. He also saw that when the price was high, those involved in the business flew high. There was an exhilaration and intrigue associated with trading coffee, according to Adem, that made him interested in the world of business.

His early impressions are probably the reason why he is in business today. According to Adem, "If you are raised by a father who is a businessman, you will probably develop an interest in doing business; if, on the other hand, you are raised by a father who is into mechanics, then you might gravitate toward a profession as a mechanic, and so on." Adem's case followed suit, although he would not become a coffee trader himself, he became a businessman and a trader, but one who trades goods in a retail shop.

Adem's mother was also in business: She operated a small coffee retail shop in Dodola and bought and sold coffee. It was good that she developed business skills, as it turns out, because Adem's father died when Adem was young and his mother had to fend for herself.

When Adem's father died, so did much of the joy of life. His father died when he was seven. His last wishes were for Adem to be raised by his uncles to enable him to acquire the essential skills and knowledge of an Ethiopian man. Therefore, he was sent to Dilla, Sidamo to live with his uncles. Though he only stayed with his uncles for four years before his mother took him back to live with her in area where he was born, he was in Dilla long enough to get a feel for the coffee trade.

Adem continued his schooling while under in his mother's watchful care, and he did well. As a result, he received a four-year scholarship from the government to attend a technical high school in Addis Ababa. The scholarship, Adem explained, included free education, free books, and a monthly stipend of 15 Birr (equivalent to $7.50). This was a lot of money in Ethiopia at the time, which was fortunate because his mother was barely getting by and couldn't afford to support him financially.

Adem continued to excel in school and moved onto the next level. In 1972, he graduated from vocational school with a diploma in auto mechanics, and received a job at the Ministry of Mines and Energy, where he worked for four years. He then left the ministry to join Ethiopian Airlines, where he worked as a mechanic until 1980, until he left Ethiopia.

When the revolution of 1974 hit, it hit Adem and his family hard. Private business was restricted and most of the coffee trade was run by a state owned company, which controlled coffee trade to the farm gate level. He didn't feel his job at the state owned airlines was secure either, and living under the reign of terror meant that he could be a victim at any time. So, he like many other young Ethiopians at the time departed Ethiopia, in search of better life. He first went to work in Saudi Arabia in 1980, but only lasted six weeks because life was so hard there. He had few choices in the labor market there: Either he could work as a manual laborer or as a sheepherder. Neither suited him.

In Pursuit of the American Dream

Adem, like many other young Ethiopians, looked to America as the place to make his dreams come true. He came to the U.S. in 1980 and applied for political asylum. The process of getting asylum status, however, proved to be arduous one. America was the place to be, but how to get to stay there was another matter. He managed to get to America on a tourist visa, but he only had $500 to his name. Once in America, he had no contacts, no information, and nowhere to turn— but at least he was in America.

He didn't know how to seek asylum status in the U.S., and he didn't know other Ethiopians who had succeeded in obtaining asylum status either. Those who knew about the U.S. immigration system told him that the process would take him many years, and even then, he might not be granted a visa. So, he had to figure it out on his own. The most difficult part of the application process, Adem recalls, was producing written supporting documents of the injustices he endured under the Derg regime. While it was true that he had endured oppression and persecuted under the regime, he didn't have any written proof of it. According to Adem, "To this day I don't know of any government that abuses and represses it citizens and then provides written documents of the injustices they commit against their citizens." All Adem could do therefore was to tell it like it was and to hope for the best.

When Adem first applied for asylum status in 1980, he didn't speak English well, nor did he understand the petitioning process well enough to succeed in the process. As a result, his application was denied in 1980. It was devastating but Adem wasn't prepared to give up. He appealed his case, and although it took him five years of waiting to get a hearing, he persisted, and ultimately prevailed.

The good thing back in the early 1980s was that asylum status seekers were issued temporary work permits while waiting for the decision. Adem said, "I benefited from the immigration system that was in place. By contrast, today, one has to wait until asylum is granted before a work permit can be issued." While Adem's case was in process, he was issued a work permit that enabled him to work throughout the waiting period.

In 1986, after waiting five years, his case was finally scheduled for a hearing and this time he hired a lawyer to prepare his case. This did not solve his problems it turns out. Unfortunately, the lawyer he hired ripped him off and stole his money without preparing the case. This was a major blow. As Adem explains, "Money was hard to come by at the time and I had a wife and daughter to support, nevertheless, I had no choice but to hire another lawyer with the little money I had left."

Finally, Adem got lucky. On the very day of the hearing, just as he and his lawyer sat down at the court, the judge announced that President Ronald Reagan was about to sign an amnesty bill that morning at 9:00 am. The judge advised them to wait for the bill to be signed, and of course they waited. They were glad that they did because, as Adem recounts, "After President Regan's signed the bill, the judge gave me the option to proceed with my case or apply for amnesty. I chose the latter and was granted permanent resident status."

A New Lease On Life

With training and experience as a mechanic under his belt, Adem was ready to settle into his profession in America. For a short while he was able to work as a mechanic for an Ethiopian who had a car body shop in Washington, DC. "He provided me with tools and I paid him half of what I made. It was good arrangement at the time," Adem notes. Conscious that his immigration petition might fail, he decided it would be wise to quit his job and spend his time acquiring more education, just in case his petition was denied and he had to return to Ethiopia.

Adem didn't have the luxury of just attending school; he had to earn some money to support his family that would soon arrive from Ethiopia. He worked as a security guard for seven months until his wife and daughter arrived from Ethiopia, at which point he sought more substantial employment. While he had hoped to get a better job as a mechanic, in fact, the best job he could find was as a parking lot attendant at Colonial Parking. He worked there at night and on weekends, while taking classes during the weekdays at the University of the District of Columbia (UDC).

Adem explains, "My wife also got a job at Highs, (which was taken over by 7-Eleven in the late eighties), where she worked during the day. During the evenings she took classes in accounting at UDC. Our daily routine was: "In the morning my wife went to work first while I took our daughter Lula to kindergarten. I also picked her up before going off to work on the night shift, while my wife went to class. We were in constant motion. It was stressful but it was leading somewhere, so we forged ahead."

Things gradually began to look more promising for Adem and his family, and in 1987, they took a significant step in realizing the American dream of homeownership. A lot of things were going on in that year for Adem and his wife: His wife was pregnant when the time came for her to take her final exams, but she succeeded and was awarded a BA in accounting, and soon after, she gave birth to their son Yusuf. They were proud that they managed everything so well, Adem recalls.

Down To Business

It wasn't all smooth sailing, however. Adem's dreams of getting a job as a professional went unrealized so he had no choice but to continue working at the parking lot until he could save enough money to start his own business. Fortunately, as he explained, "My wife also wanted to go into business and shared my view that that we would be better off if we worked for ourselves."

It took a few years before they were able to go into business, and in the meantime, Adem finished his undergraduate degree in engineering in 1989. Their plan about how to launch into business entailed his wife quitting her job, while Adem continued to work at Colonial Parking. Their first business venture, in 1992, was the ownership of a 7-Eleven, which Adem's wife managed.

Adem and his wife had a good strategy and each did their share to make their business a success. Adem notes, "My knowledge of engineering came in handy when it came time to remodel our store. My wife's work experience in a convenience store, by contrast, was the key to managing our business. By working at Highs until 1989, and later at 7-Eleven, as a sales person and manager, she learned about how to handle employees, inventory management, and other key operational issues. Her degree in accounting enabled her to handle the books as well."

Despite all of their preparation and desire to go into business, they may not have been able to realize their dream had it not been for a little luck. Their luck came in the form of Mr. Yuen, an Asian American man, who made all of the difference in their lives. Mr. Yuen, in turns out, had a number of gas stations and convenience stores in Maryland and Washington DC, one of which was in Landover Hills, MD, the area where Adem and his wife wanted to locate their own convenience store. Mr. Yuen's building had a gas station and a convenience store, but the store was separated form the gas station. Adem believed that if the store and the gas station service were integrated, it would provide a one-stop service for customers. With this vision in mind, Adem approached Mr. Yuen to make a deal. As he explains, "I approached Mr. Yuen with our business idea and as a result, he offered to let us to run his gas station for a $2,500-a-month management fee and to own the store business for ourselves."

Adem was able to convey just how good a deal it was for all concerned by showing Mr. Yuen that it was in his interest to let Adem and his wife take over the entire property and to integrate the store with the gas station. This would save Mr. Yuen money in the end and at the same time, he would benefit from the growth in the business that would undoubtedly occur once the properties were integrated.

"Mr. Yuen allowed me to tear down the wall separating the gas station office and the store and to convert the space into one business location," Adem said. With that, Adem and his wife took over the management of the gas station and ran the store at the same time.

Adem and his wife were able to finance their business through the $16,000 his wife received from cashing out her profit sharing contract she had gotten from 7-Evelen. Adem also says, "We also sold our house, bought a new one, and used our new house as collateral to raise additional capital of $38,000. All together, we started our business with $54,000 start-up capital." As planned, his wife ran the business while Adem continued to work for Colonial Parking, where he rose to the position of Manager of Operations.

Total Immersion

There is a lot to learn about doing business in America and Adem and his wife wanted to start their business in the correct way. As he said, "Although my wife graduated in accounting, when we started our first store we decided to hire an accounting firm, at a cost of $400 a month, to close our accounts, to prepare payrolls, and file tax reports. This helped us to understand where we stood financially and to start off on a good foot. It also helped us to ensure that we complied with the various legal requirements."Adem underscores that it was important to have the proper advice and not to make the mistake of trying to cut corners in terms of regulatory compliance matters.

Things go wrong even with the best planning and best advice, Adem soon learned. The problem he faced was that there were some outstanding licensing and standard requirements that Mr. Yuen had to meet before the gas station could provide service. Addressing these issues, as Adem explained, entailed a process that took over six months to resolve. "In the meantime, it harmed our ability to make the kinds of returns we anticipated. It also came as a surprise that the foot traffic we had anticipated was less than expected primarily because people in the neighborhood hadn't yet come to know that we were running a store in that location."

At this point things looked pretty bleak and they began to run into financial difficulties. Sales were slow and they began to hemorrhage money. "It was a scary time for my wife and I because we began to fear that we may lose our house. We were working 16 hours a day; yet, we could not attract enough customers to cover our costs. We ran out of working capital and didn't have any more savings we could tap into. We did not want to give up but we had very limited options on which to draw to reverse our situation. The options we saw at the time were either to close the store or for me to quit my job at Colonial Parking in order to get the profit-sharing payment cash out my profit sharing agreement. So I quit my job and got $7,000, which we used to buy inventory for our store."

"Quitting my job, however, didn't bring a lasting solution," Adem says. "The new capital we injected into our business soon dried up and within a couple of months, we were looking for financing again."

Even though things looked bleak, and Adem and his wife didn't know where to turn, they were determined not to give up on their dream and their business. "Fortunately for us, Mr. Yuen was a very understanding and supporting person, so much so that he paid $15,000 for our opening inventory, and $55,000 for setting up the equipment, all free of interest," Adem explained. Mr. Yuen's support enabled them to maintain their inventory and stay in business. In fact, without his support, Adem says, it would have been impossible for them to stay in business. Finally, after six months, when the gas station became operational, the customers they had been waiting for arrived. Within a year, Adem says, they began paying back their loan from Mr. Yuen; five years later, they totally repaid their loan.

Finally A Dream Come True

Success finally came for Adem and his wife. When it did, one of the first things they did was to expand their business and add more stores. Mr. Yuen again played an important role in their success. It was he who led the way for their future expansion by asking them to run another store he owned in Washington, DC.

"The new property had three different businesses: the smaller one was used as a store and an office to run the gas station; the second one was used for a check cashing business; and a Chinese carry-out restaurant operated in a third section," explained Adem. It didn't take Adem long to spot yet another growth opportunity. This time, he realized that the section used for the check-cashing business took up more space than the business warranted. Adem knew that his business would generate more revenue, so he offered to switch locations with the check cashing business, whose space was twice the size of his own.

Mr. Yuen supported the idea and they closed the deal. The positive results were immediate. As Adem explains, "In our previous location we were selling soft drinks and a few other items and our daily sales rarely exceeded $500. After we moved, our daily sales quadrupled and the range of products we were able to offer multiplied several times. Furthermore, by moving into the new space, we only had to pay Mr. Yuen a flat rate of $1,800 a month versus the sales commission arrangement that we had previously. In the case of the check cashing business, the owner was able to save $1,200 monthly with greater business opportunity and it was a win-win situation for all."

Once things were on a solid footing, Adem and his wife agreed that she could handle the business with the help of managers they hired and that Adem should return to his work at Colonial Parking. Adem, though now back with the parking company, remains a key player in the business. The business is going well, so well that Adem was offered yet another opportunity to expand his business, this time to operate a store in an apartment building, in Temple Hills, Maryland. "The owners, as Adem explains, proposed that we run the store for six months on a trial basis free of rent. "If we were successful they would later charge us $300 a month," Adem says. He and his wife assessed the business opportunity and they agreed to take over the store. Now they have three convenience stores, with eleven employees, and revenues of up to one million dollars annually.

Behind the Success

Reflecting on their success, Adem is quick to credit both Mr. Yuen and his wife. As for his own contribution, he is particularly proud that he was able to apply his engineering skills to remodeling his various premises. In the end, all of his training in engineering came to a good use, but not in the way he had expected. He expected to be working for someone else; instead, he wound up working for himself and employing others. Adem's is a happy story all the way around. Their daughter Lula was able to earn her Bachelor's degree in Psychology from West Virginia University and her Masters degree in Public Communication from American University. She is currently employed, as a Human Resources Representative for USAir and their son Yusuf Adem is a currently a sophomore at St. John's Military Academy in Washington, DC.

In accounting for his success in business, Adem, credits his biggest supporter Mr. Yuen. Adem and his wife didn't have to rely on external financing from private banks or government supported loans such as the U.S. Small Business Administration (SBA) loan. In fact, Adem says that he was put off from approaching the SBA for a loan because one of his friends told him a bad story about how long it had taken for him to obtain a SBA loan. In retrospect, however, he believes that it is wise to fully assess all financing options to ensure that a lack of capital doesn't prevent sound business judgment and decisions.

Words of Wisdom

The advisability of seeking external financing is underscored when Adem explains: "When we started our business, we used all of our resources to purchase inventory and undertake renovations. We expected our business to expand quickly but that didn't happen: we became cash-strapped and had to borrow an additional $70,000 dollars, at different times, from Mr. Yuen." Adem was lucky though because he could count on Mr. Yuen, but everyone doesn't have such a "Godfather." Adem learned a lesson from his experience, which is: "When one starts a business, it is important to have adequate financial resources. You need to have a backup plan in case your business does not take off as you expect it to. Developing a business takes time, and in the meantime, you need money."

Adem learned others lessons along the way. For instance, he learned that he placed too much trust in his employees. Consequently, his employees robbed them twice because he gave them unlimited access to the cash register.

He also learned that before starting a business, entrepreneurs should learn about the business first. Most importantly, he notes, one has to be able to realistically assess demand and to figure out how to win customers. Additionally, he states: "I also cannot overemphasize the importance of having the right location."

Last, but not least, he underscores the importance of being committed to the business once it is started. In his case, he says, "If we didn't persevere during the first few years and difficult times, we wouldn't be where we are today."

Zewditu (Zed) Wondemu
Owner and President
Zed's Ethiopian Restaurant
Washington, DC

Zewditu (Zed) Wondemu, born in 1953 in Addis Ababa, has played an instrumental role in introducing Ethiopian cuisine to America. As the owner and manager of Zed's Ethiopian Restaurant, located in the upscale Georgetown area of Washington, DC for the past 16 years, she has helped to ensure that Ethiopian cuisine is placed on par with the finest cuisines in the world.

Zed has fought hard to elevate the status of Ethiopian cuisine, and it has been an up hill battle most of the way. Ethiopia, after all, was not famous in America for its cuisine. To the contrary, Americans knew more about famine in Ethiopia than about its cuisine, even though it is a cuisine that has been perfected over hundreds of years.

Inch by inch and day-by-day over the years, Zed fought through the Restaurant Association, and other institutions, to ensure that food critics reviewed her cuisine. Finally, they relented and could no longer deny that Ethiopian cuisine was among the finest in the world.

Today, there are long lines outside of Zed's restaurant, and when patrons of the famous five star Four Season's Hotel, across the street from Zed's, are considering which restaurant to choose for fine dining, they only have to look across the street to see Zed's full house, or read "Zagat's" to conclude that Zed's Restaurant is among the best to choose. Zed's is unique and its food is excellent, as the critics confirm. It is not surprising therefore that when you enter her restaurant you see photos of her with President of the U.S., with First Ladies, with famous Hollywood stars, and with other famous people who have dined at Zed's.

Zed's restaurant is not located in "Little Ethiopia" in the Adams Morgan area of Washington, DC, or in the emerging "Little Ethiopia" of U Street, where most of the other Ethiopian restaurants are located. Though located in another part of town, Zed was a pioneer in the Ethiopian restaurant business in Washington, DC, and has had an impact on popularizing Ethiopian cuisine throughout the city.

Zed's accomplishments as a restaurateur stand out in a number of regards: Not only is she a trailblazer who succeeded in elevating the stature of Ethiopian cuisine in the hearts and minds of food critics and patrons alike; she is one of the few female restaurant proprietors among Ethiopians, and one of the first Ethiopian restaurateurs in Washington, DC in 1988.

Most notably, Zed's is distinguished from other Ethiopian restaurants not only because of her Georgetown location, but also because she is competing in Georgetown with many other ethnic restaurants and fine dining establishments.

There are many aspects of Zed's personal experience that differs from other Ethiopians in Washington. For one thing, unlike other Ethiopians who have immigrated to the U.S. after the Ethiopian revolution, Zed attended high school in the U.S. and feels very much a part of the American culture.

Her success in the restaurant business is also unusual because of her personal background. For one thing, she was not in the food business prior to opening her restaurant. Secondly, unlike many other restaurant owners, she earned her undergraduate and graduate degrees in America.

Prior to going into the restaurant business she worked in an unrelated business, which was for the *Great West Life* insurance, where she worked as an assistant manager for eight years. Her only preparation for the restaurant business was the experience she had operating a small coffee shop while working for *Great West Life*, which was not very much preparation, she would be the first to admit. It was enough exposure, however, to give her the idea of branching out into the restaurant business.

Zed's upbringing in Ethiopia gave no clues that she might one day become a business owner in America. Zed is from a middle class family that had the financial wherewithal to send her to the best schools, not only in America, but also in England. The plan was for her to complete high school in England, but she found both the social and weather climate to be disagreeable. Instead, she completed high school in the Maryland in the U.S. She went on to complete her university studies at Bowie State University in Maryland, where she earned undergraduate degrees in social work and psychology in 1974. The plan was also for her to return home after completing her studies, but things didn't work out according to plan.

The Revolution in Ethiopia Didn't Leave a Good Taste in Her Mouth

In 1974, Zed's father's business, like that of other businesses owned by Ethiopians, was nationalized. As the country gradually slid into political turmoil her dreams of returning began to fade. She held onto the dream of returning home as long as she could until she could no longer deny the reality of the situation at home. She kept her luggage packed for three months, hoping that the Derg takeover would be temporary. As Zed noted, "I called home often to seek advice from my parents on what to do; they advised me to stay in the United States until the situation improved. But the situation never improved and I remained in the U.S."

Upon reflection, Zed says that given what happened in Ethiopia during those years of turmoil, she is glad that she didn't return because she could have been killed or jailed. She knows that many people languished for years in jail or perished because they were opposed the regime in power. She stated, "As I did not support the government's policy, I know I too would have been imprisoned or worse."

Zed also notes, "Attending school and living in America made me appreciate the values of individual freedom, free enterprise, and an individual's right to pursue his or her own dreams. I couldn't imagine living under the Derg's communist ideology and policies where individual freedom, creativity, and dreams were stifled."

As Zed decided to stay in the U.S., she had to get a job to support herself. She went back to her school and explained the situation because of what was happening in her country and asked the President of the College to give her a job. She was lucky that the President of Bowie College understood her plight and gave her first job at the college. She explained, "I worked at the college for three years, but I was very ambitious and wanted to make more money, so I also worked for another private company on the side." Zed also notes that this didn't deter her from completing her graduate studies on time in 1977.

Although Zed's master's degree is in education, she was never able to use it in the way she might have expected. She worked for the *Great West Life* investment and insurance company upon graduating, for eight and half years for the company until she started her own restaurant. She is reflective about how her life turned out, and noted: "Things do not always happen as you plan; rather you discover your destiny in the process."

Manifest Destiny

The choice of going into the restaurant business, though it was an unrelated business to her professional background, became a logical one when so many Ethiopians began arriving in the U.S. in the early 1980s. More Ethiopians meant more demand for Ethiopian food, Zed calculated. It was a small leap of faith for her to believe that there would be a demand for Ethiopian cuisine among non-Ethiopians as well.

Although the core menu offered at Zed's is similar to that offered at other Ethiopian restaurants, what distinguishes Zed's is the ambience of her restaurant, the quality of her food, and her participation and charm as the proprietor. You can go to her restaurant any day of the week and you will find her there, night and day. She will greet you, serve you, advise you, and make you feel at home with her Ethiopian hospitality. Once you have had the Zed dining experience, you always return.

Famous food critics agree that although the menus at Ethiopian restaurants are similar, Zed's restaurant is distinguished from the rest. As Robert Shoffer mentioned in his review of Zed's restaurant in the "Washingtonian" magazine: "At Zed's you'll sample Ethiopia's culinary repertory at its best: The sauces of its wats are more concentrated in flavor; its alechas more complexly seasoned; and the injure—a crepe like bread that, in lieu of tableware, is torn into small swatches to pick up morsels of food—is wonderfully light. This fine kitchen offers a few specialties and the best is cubes of beef stewed with collard greens."

An Entrepreneurial Streak

When you dig deeper into Zed's background, perhaps it is not so surprising after all that she wound up choosing the path of entrepreneurship.

Zed is an Amhara, and business was not a path that many Amharas chose when she was growing up in Ethiopia because of the lower social status that was accorded to trade and business. Despite the social stigma associated with being in business, Zed's father chose the path of entrepreneurship. It wasn't an easy choice for him, Zed explains. As she recalls, "My father's peers were in public service and he was expected to follow suit. Emperor Haile Selassie himself offered my father a position in the civil service but my father opted instead to join the private sector."

Her father had a number of businesses: a liquor store, a farm on which he farmed *teff* (grain that grows in Ethiopia) and maize; a wholesale distributorship of liquor; and a cement distribution business. "He was a hard-working, smart, and enlightened father. He was my role model and I was his favorite," Zed says.

Zed learned a lot from her father, but as she notes, she was too young to be his apprentice. Nevertheless, she learned valuable lessons from observing him in business and has drawn on these from memory for guidance in her own business. Zed also notes, "Interestingly, however, my father would have been very disappointed to see me running a restaurant. He had invested a lot of money in me, and in his mind, he was grooming me to get into a respectable profession, such as being a medical doctor, lawyer, or an educator. The last profession he would have chosen for me is business—not because of a gender bias, but because he knew firsthand how hard it was to operate a business and he wanted an easier life for me."

When something forms a part of one's early childhood impressions, it is hard to erase that memory. For Zed, entrepreneurship was in her blood. As she explained, "Even though I was in a comfortable job, something stirred in me to lead me to start my own business, she says. "It was a calling and I had no choice," according to Zed.

Heeding the Call

The first thing Zed did when she decided to go into business was to consult with her husband to ascertain whether he would support her—not financially, but emotionally. Her strategy was to start a small business on the side while keeping her "day job." Zed explains, "my husband supported my idea, and in fact, it was he who first spotted a building that would be suitable for her to lease. He was driving around in the city when he came across a sign advertising a building for lease. He immediately thought of my interest to start a coffee shop and encouraged me to go after it. The next day we went together and checked out the premises and struck a deal with the building manager, not for that particular space, as it turned out, but for a more suitable one," Zed says. Knowing that she had her husband's full support, Zed took the lease and embarked on a path of entrepreneurship.

Her husband supported her throughout; he helped outfit the premises and assisted her in undertaking a survey to assess the needs of the neighborhood, according to Zed. Based on the responses to her survey, Zed concluded that a coffee shop would be a good business at the location, so she opened her first coffee shop in the office building. "I also sold magazines, newspapers, and other items for office people," Zed notes.

The first thing Zed had to do to get started was to hire someone. She said, "I hired a woman to run my coffee shop who was very honest and trustworthy, and she gave me all my money at the end of every business day." Incredibly it was around $600 and $700 a day from that little shop of only 300 square feet. My monthly rental expense was only $250 a month and I had no other major expenses. The business was so lucrative that I established another one. All the while I continued working full-time for *Great West Life*," Zed said.

Zed had some good fortune too, which made a world of difference in her plans. She said, "While operating my coffee shops, I met an Ethiopian woman who was a very good cook who I used to hire her from time to time to prepare Ethiopian food for my parties at home. She was a really talented cook and I believed that with her skill and my drive, we could do something together. She became an anchor when I opened my first restaurant in 1988."

Although off to a good start, it took some time for Zed to really believe that she was in business. As she said, "My intention was to continue for the investment and insurance company, as I had previously done." Life intervened, however. After one year, the lady on whose cooking talent she had depended quit because she found the job to be too demanding. Zed notes that at this point, "there was still a long way to go to make my restaurant successful." She was dismayed that the woman on whom she depended just gave up and quit.

When the going gets tough…Luckily, Zed explains, "I am a good cook myself, so I pitched in as a 'chief cook', manager, and CEO. I soon learned that the restaurant business is time-consuming, complex, demanding, and something that I could not do on the side." As the pressure to manage the restaurant increased, she had to make a choice: Quit her job and manage the business full time, or throw away all the money she had invested. She chose wisely: She quit her job and began working full-time in her restaurant.

A lot was at stake. As Zed recalls, "I had already invested a significant amount of money and energy in putting the business together and I didn't want to give at this point; I had no choice but to forge ahead." She adds, "Although I was now devoting all of my time to the business, my actual intention was to get the restaurant going and to return to my 'day job.'" The problem was that it took a long time to get the business going. In fact, it took four years to get the restaurant on a solid footing, and by this time, it was too late to return to her job. She realized that her business was her job.

From Ground Zero

Zed had to come to grips with the fact that she was now a full time, 100 percent restaurant business owner, and that it was up to her to "make it or break it." She chose to make it. As she explains, "I did it all from scratch: I saved my own funds to start the restaurant and I grew the customer base from scratch."

She found, however, that there was one thing she couldn't do on her own: Figure out the legal requirements for operating a restaurant in America. One of the major hurdles to cross, as she explains, was acquiring a Food Inspection Certificate, which is issued by the Department of Health's (DOH) Food Protection Division. Zed further explained that restaurants must also have a certified food supervisor on the premises at all times when the restaurant is open to the public. The requirements don't stop there. One of the most challenging ones, Zed says, is obtaining an Alcoholic Beverage Regulation Administration (ABRA) license. There is more: "If you serve food on the premises, you must also obtain a Public Health Food Establishment Restaurant Endorsement," Zed notes. Finally, food establishments must have regular rodent control inspections, and in this area, her husband's knowledge and training came in handy. He had previously worked in Kentucky as a health inspector, Zeds says.

Once fully immersed in the restaurant business, Zed had a chance to reflect and to realize that it was a huge leap from owning a small coffee shop to being a full fledged restaurant owner. She explained, "It took years to come to grips with my new life as a restaurant owner. Yes, I had wanted to own a restaurant, but the reality of running a restaurant business is far less glamorous than its image," Zed says. For years, I always dreamed of going back to my old job," she adds.

Of all the regulatory hurdles Zed had to cross in building her business, none was more challenging than obtaining a liquor license. Zed explains, "It is a process that takes months, so I had to operate my restaurant without having a liquor license for six months." Getting a license is by no means guaranteed, however. Zed said: "I was lucky that I was able to get a liquor license at all because after mine was granted, a moratorium was placed in Georgetown on granting any new liquor licenses. Consequently, new restaurant owners have to purchase existing licenses, which can cost between $40,000 to $120,000, depending on the type of license," Zed explains.

Zed credits the Ethiopian community for keeping her afloat in the period before she could obtain her liquor license. As she said, "During the period that we endured without a liquor license, it was my Ethiopian compatriots' patronage that I counted on, and which made the difference in enabling me to weather the storm. Ethiopian taxi drivers were especially supportive—I wish there was a better way to express my appreciation for the critical support they gave me in the early stages. Even now, many people from our community, some of whom don't even know who I am, have been very supportive, and I am very grateful for that."

Zed notes that support from her Ethiopian compatriots was meaningful to her in other ways as well. "The support of the Ethiopian community was especially meaningful for me not just because of the benefit to my business, but also because I came to the U.S. when I was only 15 years old and I didn't have a chance to build my own social base among other Ethiopians. My roots were very shallow in the Ethiopian community. The restaurant business forced me to create deeper roots in the Ethiopian community." At the same time, because she grew up in America, she felt comfortable with the system, even when it seemed so daunting when she was going through the compliance process for her restaurant.

On Being an American

Zed completed high school, undergraduate, and graduate degrees in the U.S.; she has grown up in the American culture. As there were few Ethiopians around her at the time, her roots are in the mainstream culture. "When you go to high school in a country, you think of yourself as belonging to that country. I went to high school in America, obtained my universities degrees here, and got my first job here. I am a U.S. citizen, not just in terms of naturalization, but also in terms of the way I feel."

Zed thinks that having a "foreign name" like hers may have put her in a disadvantaged position. She explains, "Lets say I need a loan of half a million dollars now. Even with all of my business experience and my educational background, I would probably be scrutinized more than someone with the last name of "Johnson." I often tell my friends may be I should have taken my husband's last name, Gabriel, which is more neutral. It is not in our culture to take our husbands' last names, however.

On the issue of accessing government backed financing programs, Zed has been disappointed because of what she considers to be the high cost of accessing such financing. As she explained, "I met a lady from the Overseas Private Investment Corporation (OPIC) who explained the kind of support and services that OPIC can give to those who are interested in doing business in developing countries. I asked her if I was an eligible applicant, as I have a plan to do business in Ethiopia. She said that I was eligible. However, when I tried to fill the application form upon my return, I found the service fees charged by the OPIC to be too high for a small business owner like me. They charge all kinds of fees and I didn't find their terms attractive or encouraging. They also ask you to provide a great deal of collateral to qualify for their loans. If I put all that collateral down then why don't I just go through the normal bank process? The interest rate they offered was not that great either. While I have retained the application, it is doubtful that I'll ever call on OPIC to support any investment I might make in Ethiopia in the future."

At the same time, Zed is quick to admit that she needs to devote more time to more fully acquaint herself with the various financing opportunities that might be available for small businesses like hers.

On the subject of social capital, Zed is clear. She knows about the power of networking and business advocacy, and is a member of various business associations and Chambers of Commerce in her area. Not surprisingly she stated: "Perhaps because there were many times when I was treated as an outsider, although I felt like a 'belonger' on the inside, I put a lot of stock into belonging to various associations that I believe are important. For instance, I am member of the Metro Washington Restaurants Association, and a member of its board for ten years. I also served as the chairperson of the association. Currently I am a board member of the National Restaurants Association, which is a very big association. Many big hotels, such as Marriott, and many large restaurants are members of the association. I am probably the smallest business in the association. I am very privileged to be a board member of such an association.

I am also a member of the Washington DC Convention Centers Association, and the Independent Restaurant Owners Association. Zed is also active in a number of non-profit organizations. "I am a member of the Ethiopian American Constituency (EAC), whose goal is to serve as an advocacy group for its constituency by actively participating in the election process. I am also a member of the *Montgomery County Resource Bank,* a databank of various professional background and businesspersons. Whenever they ask me to teach in the classroom for a half a day, I volunteer my time to give motivational speeches at high schools."

Zed has many accomplishments she can point to regarding her community involvement but one that she is most proud of, she explains, is to have been part of an initiative of the Restaurant and Hotel Association to establish the Charter High School of Washington, DC. The school focuses on preparing students to enter the hospitality trades and Zed serves as the Vice Chair of the Hotel and Restaurant Hospitality Foundation that established the charter high school. She was involved in raising funds from restaurants and hotels in the area to finance the high school. Zed is proud to note that Mr. Marriott, of the Marriott Hotels, for instance, donated $1 million to the high school. Zed is also involved in the community through contributing to various charitable causes through her restaurant. For instance, she said, "we gave food to two hundred volunteers who worked for the Red Cross after the tragedy of September 11. We also supported Ethiopians who were working to raise funds to support the fight against hunger in Ethiopia and continue to look for ways to be active in the community and to make a contribution whenever we can."

Networking Among Ethiopian Restaurants

Zed believes that Ethiopian restaurant owners have more power than they realize. If they effectively ban together, they could leverage their strengths to influence public policies that affect their businesses, according to Zed. On her part, she is an advocate of creating an Ethiopian Restaurant Owners Association to enable Ethiopian restaurateurs to work more effectively together." In her view, such an association could be instrumental in promoting Ethiopian cuisine and in serving as a voice for issues that affects them, such as security, licensing and regulations. They could also learn from each other about how to stay competitive in the market.

There are many issues that need to be addressed in the Ethiopian restaurant community. For instance, Zed explains, "Preparing Ethiopian food is very labor intensive because of the number of spices involved that have to be prepared for each dish. The people working in our kitchens and in the restaurants work really hard chopping, peeling, simmering, and stewing. However, we don't charge prices as high as other mainstream restaurants, such as French, Italian, or similar restaurants, even though there may be more work involved in the case of preparing Ethiopian food," Zed also knows that there is also another side of the equation, which is food promotion and marketing. She believes that Ethiopian restaurateurs don't place enough effort in this regard. As she says, "We must ban together to raise the awareness of our cuisine, to diversify our menus, to educate the public about our cuisine, and to develop the skills of our workers. We are, after all, Ambassadors of our culture through our cuisine."

We are also integrated into the communities where we are located. For instance, "Interestingly, depending on the season, I have anywhere from twenty to twenty-five employees of diverse cultural backgrounds working in my restaurant; some are Ethiopian-Americans, some are Hispanics, and some are Asians," Zed notes. We also outsource some of our administrative work such as our payroll and accounting services, cleaning, linen, etc. We are part of the community and the community is part of us."

Importance of Family Support

"Even though none of my family members work in my restaurant, they understand my work and the pressure it puts on me, and they try not to add any more pressure on me," Zed states. Her husband has been a great help to her. She said, "My husband is very handy: Whenever I don't want to pay for services to fix something, I just ask my husband and he will fix it for me. For instance, my computer was having some problems recently and he came and fixed it for me. I have purchased new equipment for my restaurant and he is going to put it together."

Zed's children, ages 17 and 14, are still in school and don't work in the restaurant but they share in many other activities together. Zed noticed that her daughter has an entrepreneurial streak like her: She has already written her own cookbook, which is published and sold in Zed's restaurant. Zed is hopeful that she will take over the business one day. As for her son, Zed doesn't know what career path her son might take, but he is fluent in Japanese and recently lived in Japan for a short while. Whatever her children decide to do, Zed and her husband will be behind them 100 percent.

Advice to Emerging Entrepreneurs

The advice Zed gives is heartfelt and from the depth of her experience. She explains, "When I started my restaurant I didn't fully embrace it—I didn't really feel it, smell it, nor was I in full synchronicity with it. My attention was diverted: I kept thinking that I was going back to my job. It took me some time before I could finally convince myself that this is the business that I wanted to do and this is the country where I wanted to live. I missed a once and a lifetime opportunity to really embrace my business from the very start and you never get that again.

Based on her experience, Zed advises newly emerging entrepreneurs to be sure of what they are doing and to do it with their whole heart, whatever it is. She adds, "I also wish I had consulted people with experience in the restaurant business. One has to be mature enough to seek and internalize advice from other people. I am lucky that I succeeded regardless, but if you start a new business, it is important to get advice from people who know more about the industry than yourself." Zed gives an example: "Believe it or not, I really didn't even know about the need to get a liquor license before starting the restaurant. Can you imagine the financial impact on my business that being unable to obtain a liquor license would have had?"

Zed also advises that it is important for potential entrepreneurs to prepare themselves with the knowledge of what it takes to run the business before leaping into entrepreneurship. Specifically, she advises, "The best way to get such knowledge is to work in a similar business. If you want to open a restaurant, you need to work in a restaurant to understand what it takes. If you want to open a pizza place, go and find a job in a pizza place, and if you want to open a restaurant, you should work in a restaurant to get the exposure needed to fully understand the business from the inside out. In short, know what you are getting yourself involved in before taking the plunge. In a word, be "smart" before you go into business, and look before you leap."

Girma Kassa Desta
President
Adams Morgan Hardware, Inc.
Washington, DC

G irma was born in 1950 in the small town of Debre Berhan, in the province of Shewa, about 60 miles north of Addis Ababa. His father, who fought against the Italian occupation of 1935-1941, was a war hero who later became a police officer and served in various parts of Shewa province. Girma was the only child of his father who raised him by himself for the first few years of his childhood, until he remarried.

As a war hero, Girma's father was granted a plot of land; that was the good news. The bad news was that his land grant was near land owned by a member of the nobility who thought that Girma father's land should be his own. That person staked his claim and as a consequence, Girma's father had to spend over two decades in court, trying in vain, to reclaim his rightful grant. He fought all the way up until 1974, when the land was nationalized. For different reasons this time, he was again denied access to his land.

This injustice, and those that Girma witnessed that were perpetrated by other powerful landowners, shaped Girma's views, and ignited his social activism. His social activism, in turn, landed him in prison for eight years, where he experienced the most tortuous circumstances, where he did not see sunlight for one year, and where he was denied access to water for washing for one year. Under these circumstances, his color changed to the point that he looked like an alien.

How Girma managed to get from this set of circumstances and how he became an entrepreneur in America is no short of a miracle.

When Girma was released from prison in 1983 after eight years, he had nothing: no job, no prospects, no connections, and no help. His only way out was to get to America, which he succeeded in doing in 1985, as a student. If there was ever a case for granting refugee status, it was his, but it wasn't easy to go through the process, so instead, he came to America as a student.

Just because he landed in America, as a student did not mean he landed well. In fact, he joined the ranks of the poor and downtrodden in America, and was homeless for the first few months. Though homeless and penniless in the nation's capital, his spirit was unbroken.

A Mustard Seed of Hope

It was true that Girma experienced hardships growing up, but he never imagined how hard his life would become. At first, despite his father's unfortunate plight, he believed that his own life would work out. Unlike many Ethiopians at the time, he not only completed high school, he was able to attend the Addis Ababa Teacher Training College, from which he graduated in 1970 as a teacher.

He was also able to secure a government job as a teacher, and taught in the remote village of Minie in the Arsi province for three years. When we say remote; it was really remote, so much so that the Ministry of Education considered serving there for one year to be equivalent to serving two years in other localities. It was commonplace to find snakes in the classroom, for instance.

What was worse than the real snakes, however, were the snakes in the form of the powerful robbers and outlaws who controlled the area and the social and economic life of the local people. The outlaws also controlled what happened at the school. For instance, if any of the local churches celebrated one of the Saint's Days favored by the outlaws, Girma's school had to close, because the outlaws demanded that the teachers and students alike travel on foot for miles to attend a church service in honor of the Saint. Like the monarchy, the outlaws used the church as their power base to control the people.

Well-connected foreigners also controlled vast areas of land, and the people who lived there. Girma recalls that one foreigner named Jilaldin, who owned most of the fertile land in the area, had a coffee plantation and commercial farm. He used to force his tenants and workers to make their children available to work on his land otherwise he would evict them from the land he owned. Children were often prevented from attending school because of this tyranny. Girma recalls that in the years before the Ethiopian revolution of 1974, Jilaldin warned him and his colleagues, on the threat of death, to close the school because he feared that they were contributing to the uprising.

Girma was indeed an advocate for change, both as a student and as a teacher. At his school, he organized and led a number of activities that supported the idea of political reform in the country. He also served as the chief editor of the school's student magazine and as a chairman of the local chapter of the teacher's association. Some of his activities were strictly non-political, however, and were aimed simply at helping his fellow man. For instance, in 1973, when he was teaching in Arsi, he organized students to provide labor to the local farmers through which he raised 10,000 Birr (about $US5,000 at the time) to help drought and famine victims of Wello and Tigray.

When Haile Selassie's regime was finally overthrown in 1974, Girma soon found that he had a new battle: fighting the Derg regime, which turned out to be more oppressive than the one it replaced. He explains, "I joined the Ethiopian Teachers' Association, a trade union that actively advocated for social and political reform in the country. When the political opposition against the Derg took a more organized form, I decided to join the Ethiopian People's Revolutionary Party (EPRP), one of the political forces that opposed the new military regime." It was the last thing he did as a free person in Ethiopia. For the next eight years, from 1976 to 1983, he languished in prison because of his political activism.

Keftegna 25 Prison and Torture Palace

Girma was teaching at the Felege Yordanos junior high school in Addis Ababa when he was suddenly imprisoned. As he had been active in promoting political awareness among teachers, students, and parents, he became a target of the Derg's security forces. He came to the attention of the Derg regime when one of his fellow teachers in his school was detained and tortured by the Derg. Pressed for names of anti-Derg sympathizers the teacher gave his interrogators Girma's name, which led to Girma's detention.

Girma recalls, "When I was imprisoned in jail in Addis Ababa, no charges were brought against me. Unlike in America, where the writ of *Habeas Corpus* protects the rights of citizens and requires them to be charged with a crime if they are detained, no such protections existed in Ethiopia at the time." Girma also vividly recalls, "I was beaten almost daily, and my thighs were burned with a hot iron bar; it was so bad that I couldn't even walk to the restroom, because my feet had swollen from the beatings. The pain I had to endure was beyond any description. It was so excruciating that I wished they had finished me off in the torture chamber. The beatings didn't have any specified schedule or pattern; they would call any of us at any time, day or night, take us to the torture room and beat us until they got tired. I was lucky to survive because many others didn't make it."

Girma still finds it hard to control his emotions when he thinks of his prison; it deeply saddens him when he thinks of how many innocent people lost their lives in the torture chambers of the Derg regime. He recalls how one of his cellmates was tortured non-stop and died as a result. His name was Birhanu, and his only crime was having the misfortune of sitting next to a wanted EPRP member at a coffee bar one day. It was an unfortunate day when the Derg's securities came to arrest that man they also arrested Birhanu, who was simply in the wrong place at the wrong time. They tortured Birhanu day and night for the next two weeks until he passed away under the torture.

Girma wasn't the only one that perished; others died as well as a result of being tortured and others chose to take their own lives instead of facing the torture chamber. Girma was in Keftegna 25 prison for a year and half, during which time he was not allowed to see sunlight, and was denied water for washing. Because he couldn't wash, he explained, "My face turned yellowish and I looked like an alien. I never combed my hair, washed, or changed my clothes throughout the ordeal." He was finally transferred to a relatively better prison, where he remained for the next six and half years—all without being charged of a crime. "In 1983, I was finally considered to be harmless to the Derg, and was released," Girma said.

On the positive side, and there was one, according to Girma, "I learned many positive things from adversity. For one thing, it underscored the importance of family and friends: you can never forget the people who supported you and cared for you while you were in prison; therefore I am always grateful to my friends and family. My father died when I was in prison, but my stepmother took care of me for the whole eight years with the little resources she had. She regularly came at 4:00 am each day, having walked from Sebeta, about 20 miles outside of Addis Ababa and lugging food for me with her. Many of my friends also supported me during that most difficult time. My stepmother is now old, but I try to pay her back in my way. I also learned that no matter how grim life appears; you can survive and with a mustard seed of hope, strive and prevail to have a better life."

Free At Last

Freedom is relative. Although Girma was released from prison and the torture chamber, he was still a prisoner of the Derg's repressive regime. Worse yet, he had lost his job as a teacher and had nowhere to go. He had to live from hand to mouth and off the kindness of his family and friends. Luckily, he had friends in the United States who knew him as a teacher, and as an opposition member and were willing to help him leave the country and to come to the United States.

Girma came to the United States in 1985 on a student visa but he didn't have the financial means to actually attend school. Girma says, "When I first came to the United States, I stayed with my uncle who has since returned to Ethiopia. He was a good man at heart, but I soon learned he had a mighty temper, and as a result, I was only able to stay with him for two weeks."

Girma had nowhere to turn when he left his uncle. As he explains, "I had other relatives, but I was so heart broken that I didn't want to depend on anyone anymore. So, I chose to live on the streets. Before taking up residence on a doorstep, I spent my first night as a homeless person in a nightclub where I spent the whole night sitting, until the club closed around 2 am. When the owners made me leave the club, I returned to the apartment where my uncle lived and slept on the steps of its top floor. I reckoned that as my uncle lived on the third floor, he wouldn't see me because he wouldn't go upstairs."

"In the morning, I'd go to one of my friends, who worked at a hardware store; he would buy me breakfast, my only meal of the day. I then wandered around the city, as I had nowhere else to go" Girma recalls. "At night I returned to the steps to sleep. This was my routine for more than a month. All the while, I couldn't have made it without the help of my friend; he saved my life during this ordeal. Eventually my friend came to know that I was not staying with my uncle. When he pressed me, I finally told him that I was sleeping on the steps. At first, he was furious, but soon wondered whether I had developed some "bad habits" that would make me go out and live on the streets. When I convinced him that my only problem was poverty, he insisted that I stay with him."

126

Girma needed more than a place to live; he needed a job. "I asked my friend, who was working at a hardware store, to introduce me to his boss and he did. His boss, the owner of the hardware store, wanted to know how much I knew about hardware, and I told him honestly that I knew nothing about it, and that I had been a teacher back home. It was a difficult choice for the owner, but to sweeten the pot I offered to work for him for free for a day, on a trail basis," Girma said. "He observed that I worked nonstop and refused to take a break and that no job was too big or small for me, and he hired me on the spot and it was the beginning of my real life in America."

Once Girma got a job, he was able to start going to school, but only for a little while, because he had to work long hours to earn the money to remain in school. It soon became an untenable situation, and Girma was forced to make a choice between school and employment. He chose the latter.

Hard Work at the Hardware Store

Girma's story conveys just how hard it can be for newly adjusting immigrants. As he tells the story, "I worked so hard such that some of my compatriots who knew me in the area were worried about me. To me, however, it was a privilege to have a job and not to have to depend on anyone. Furthermore, given my life in prison, everything else was easy by comparison."

Attitude is always half of the battle, and Girma had a positive attitude about working in the hardware store. He recalls, "Everyday, I learned a lot working in the store, especially from the customers. For instance, some customers gave me advice on how to hang picture frames and how paint houses, and others explained how they used the various pipes and fittings we sold at the store. I used every opportunity to learn new ideas from my customers. For me, it was just like a university."

Girma put all of his learning to good use. He explains, "Eventually, I learned enough about home improvement to begin taking on outside jobs for clients. I started out by sanding floors and painting houses. I worked in the hardware store from eight to six after, and after work, I began my outside jobs. Before long, I was able to get my own apartment, and later, even to purchase my own home. I continued to live frugally and didn't buy a car for two years. It took a long time to get over the shock of being homeless, and I didn't want that to happen again, so I was very careful with money."

To appreciate the irony of Girma working in a hardware store, one must understand a cultural legacy of Ethiopia. Hardware, by its very nature, implies tools made of metal, objects that historically were made by blacksmiths. The interesting point is that Ethiopians living in rural areas in the past used to regard blacksmiths, and people who worked with metal, as sorcerers. Not surprisingly under the circumstances, many of the hardware tools were unknown to Girma, and their applications had no parallel in the daily lives of most Ethiopians. Therefore, there was a cultural barrier to cross in learning about the hardware that Girma was selling.

Learning the Hardware Business

Though a very common business in the United States, the hardware store business is complex and capital-intensive, and requires significant working capital. Whereas many Ethiopians have started their own businesses, very few of them have tried to get into the hardware business because of its complexities and unfamiliarity. Girma admits that he didn't grow up in an environment that gave him knowledge about hardware, so it was a lucky break that landed him in a position to be employed in a hardware store.

There was a lot that Girma needed to learn about hardware. One source of information about the tools and products of hardware stores would be previous work in the construction industry, but Girma didn't have that experience. By contrast, Hispanics are fast becoming experts in many trades in the United States. Girma comments on the differences in culture noting, "when I compare Ethiopian women and Hispanic women, I find a huge gap between the two. Among Ethiopians, women and men exchange expensive jewelry, or perfume, and other gifts on various occasions. By contrast, if the husband of a Hispanic wife works as a carpenter, his wife would buy him something that he can use in his trade for a gift, such as a saw, a measuring tape, or other tools."

"Even when we visit our homes back in Ethiopia, look at the kinds of gifts we often take jeans, sneakers, and other consumer goods, but not tools or equipment. There may be one person out of many who does so, but so far, I have never seen people take tools and equipment home as gifts. One of my goals in the future is to start a hardware business back in Ethiopia, to introduce new skills and products and to create employment opportunities."

The hardware store is not any ordinary retail business that one can jump into. With the large capital it requires to maintain stock of thousands of product types on the shelf, not many immigrants are positioned to operate a hardware store. It was a combination of focus, hard work, persistence, and a bit of luck that enabled Girma to enter the hardware business. He has also been a good saver from the start. As he explained, "Saving money is a good thing. It was because I was so frugal that when opportunity knocked for me to become a hardware store franchisee, I was financially able to take advantage of the opportunity. After I had worked in the store for five years, the owners wanted to sell it. As I was finally ready to become an entrepreneur, I asked the owners to sell me the store. At the time, the store was a franchise of Servistar and there were very few blacks involved in the franchise. Fortunately, I was accepted into the franchise, and I operated the store under the franchise system for the next three years, until a bad thing happened."

Competing in the Hardware Store Business

Girma is competing in a very difficult business, at a time when hardware stores are consolidating. What is happening in the economy also has a bearing on the fortunes of hardware stores. For instance, a buoyant national economy expands the number of "do-it-yourselfers", who in turn generate a wave of growth in the hardware/home improvement retail industry. At the same time, this leads to more competition in the market, and to a further crowding out of small hardware shops like that of Girma's.

To understand what Girma is up against, one has to look at how the home improvement retail chains, like Home Depot and Lowe's, operate and wind up winners in the process, while the smaller, mom-and-pop hardware stores have a hard time being price-competitive with their "big-box" cousins. The niche of small hardware stores remains convenience for consumers who, for instance, want to buy a box of nails without having to conduct a warehouse-wide search. In Girma's case, his hardware store is located at the corner of the popular Adams Morgan area, where all kinds of restaurants, nightclubs, and bars converge, but which is also where there is high density of potential hardware store clients.

The home improvement market is a large and growing market but the problem is, Home Depot, Lowe's, and Tru-Serv are taking up all the growth. Tru-Serv, the largest independent hardware chain, for instance has 10,500 stores with more than $4.5 billion in annual retail sales. The competition for market share between the two heavyweights in the industry, Home Depot and Lowe's, is also intense, with both chains being in the midst of aggressive national expansion campaigns through increased outlets, price cuts, and expanded product ranges. Both of them claim to have a large assortment of products, enabling them to be one-stop shopping venues.

Thus, the odds are stacked against Girma as a very small "mom and pop" shop. Nevertheless, Girma never gives up. He keeps himself up-to-date on products, and pays attention to his customers' feedback, believing that at the end of the day, customer service matters. Girma explains, "People who reside in the area of my store come from all kinds of professions, and most have advanced educational backgrounds. These are customers who demand accuracy and professionalism in the service we provide. You cannot easily persuade them to take products that are not going to work for them. Therefore, I try to anticipate their demands and to provide them with the best service I can. Because of the quality service I provide, I have been able to develop loyal customers."

Protect Me from My Friends

Girma's first instinct is to trust people and to look at things positively; traits that enduring eight years of prison life could not take away from him. When he started his hardware store, he hired an accountant who was also from Ethiopia. For Girma, things seemed to be going well, and he valued the service of his accountant very much. Little did he know that the very person he trusted would one day try to destroy his business and his life. As he recalls, "I considered my accountant my friend and trusted him implicitly to take care of all the financial reports. I also relied on his advice in other areas, and began to consider him as a part of my family. It was a bond and trust that would be my undoing, however. He plotted to, and succeeded in, stealing my store from under me."

In 1992, Girma remembers, "While plotting to take over my business, he and his family traveled with me to Ethiopia for a vacation, which was my first trip to Ethiopia since I left in 1985. We spent time together, traveled together, and we were just like one family. In the middle of our vacation, however, my friend cut short his visit to return to Washington, leaving his family back in Ethiopia with me. The reason he gave me at the time was that it would be better for him to return early to watch over the business. I never once thought that he was plotting to destroy me, and didn't give it another thought. When I returned from Ethiopia some weeks later, the situation became clear: he had stolen my business from me, through a series of financial moves and maneuvering of paperwork. As a result, I had to declare bankruptcy. When the trustee from the bankruptcy court came and closed my store down, my heart was broken and my spirit and trust in people was broken."

"After all of my hard work, my years of suffering, it was unjust, unfair, and unbelievable. I hired a lawyer to defend my case, and only then learned the extent to which my former friend was, in fact, my enemy. It turns out that my accountant had plotted to take over the store with a friend of his, another Ethiopian."

I didn't just lose the store, the most important physical asset in my life; I also lost the ability to trust, and this was a much greater loss. After having worked 12 to 13 hours a day building my business inch by inch, it was now all gone. Under such circumstances, it is a wonder that I didn't lose my mind as well."

As Girma thought about what his compatriot did to him, vengeance seemed the only solace. He said, "I decided take law into my own hands, and drove to Greenbelt, Maryland to buy a gun to end his life. I shopped around, inquired about types of guns for sell, their prices, and the requirements, if any, to buy a gun. I decided to buy one but as I was filling out the form to purchase it, I reflected on my years in prison, on the difficult times and hardships I had gone through before owning a business, and about my family background, and suddenly realized: I hadn't come to America to become a millionaire, and I don't have to end someone's life over money. As long as I was healthy and could work hard, I could start my life all over again, even if I had to work as a daily laborer."

Girma came to his sense and said, "I tore up the form, didn't buy the gun, and resolved to start all over again." But he would have to start with extremely limited and constrained financial resources, now that he was in bankruptcy. The one solace he had from his unfortunate episode is that his former accountant and his accomplice were only able to hold onto the store for four months before the city purchased the property and ordered the store to be demolished.

Back to Square One

After all he had been through, from being homeless, to working day and night in a hardware store for five years, to finally owning his own store, quite unbelievably, he was back to square one. His worst nightmare had come true. "Once again, I was jobless, but this time I had a mortgage I had to pay. My house had no furniture, and I feared that soon, at the rate I was going, I would have no house either. All I had was hope, and one friend, a 'real' friend, who helped me. He informed me about government auctions, which were instrumental in enabling me to acquire goods to sell in my current store."

It wasn't easy for Girma to get back on his feet, but he did eventually. He said, "I was able to acquire a lease for my store through a person who knew me from my previous business. He had mercy on me and gave me the lease without going through the regular procedures, and without requiring me to be on solid financial footing" Girma said.

"Despite what had happened, I was excited about my new business, which I named *Adams Morgan Hardware.* Unfortunately, however, my financial problems were so serious it was difficult to operate my business. I had insufficient working capital, and was therefore unable to build inventory. In a hardware store, there are thousands of items that you need to have. For instance, if you are selling paint and don't have paint brushes, you cannot stay in the hardware business. Customers want to buy all the items from one place or else they will turn to the competition, and the competition is formidable. There are the large franchises as well as community franchises that pose major competition to little stores like mine, and while personal relationships account for a large part of how small stores like mine can remain in business, at the end of the day, you still have to have the goods, and for that, you have to have the working capital."

"Credit cards were my salvation and answer to my working capital needs. Over time, I have been able to expand my business to its current level. In the meantime, I continue to work on improving my credit record and paying my debts. I am also trying to restore my faith in people, after having been betrayed by a person whom I considered a friend. Despite my setbacks, I have learned to be happy again. I am now married, and have two wonderful kids. The positive lesson I take from my past experience is that I can always start my life all over again. Currently, I have one full-time employee, and gross revenues of around a quarter of a million and growing. Even if I lose what I have right now, it wouldn't be the end of the world, and I know I could start over yet again."

Branching Out

"Once my feet were firmly back on the ground in my core business, I realized that I could afford to expand into new areas, so my friend and I decided to start a computer training business. We didn't have the requisite background or experience in the field, but we figured we could hire a teacher who did. Our target market was the Ethiopian community, but our lack of background and knowledge in the field was very limiting.

"Despite our limitations, we hired teachers in computer technology, both Ethiopians and non-Ethiopians, and tried to market our service to Ethiopians in the Metropolitan area. Our marketing strategy was to allow students to take classes and pay the fee on an installment basis. In the meantime, we kept paying all expenses and teachers' salaries to run the training school. Some students were conscientious enough to pay on time, but many more took advantage of our generosity and naiveté. Before our business failed, we had financed the production of Amharic software, which we were proud of, but which did not take off. In retrospect, we failed because we did not properly study the market before we jumped into business. "

"Our second failing is that we were only targeting the Ethiopian market; we failed to branch out to others outside of our community. It pays to reach out to others outside of the community. For instance, I met a policeman in my hardware store and told him about our computer training service. He said he would call me back if there were opportunities. After some months, he called me and asked if I would take 50 homeless computer trainees, explaining that the government would cover the cost. Although we had already closed our school at the time, and could not take the project, I obtained information about the project because I met this police officer."

"Meeting people outside our community is something Ethiopians should make a priority," Girma adds. "Because of my friends and acquaintances among African-Americans, Whites, and Latinos, I get information about business opportunities from time to time. By contrast, many Ethiopians focus more on political issues back home rather than on exchanging business information among our community members.

Lessons to Share

"The most important lesson I have learned is: do not start a hardware store without adequate capital. Secondly, I would advise anyone who is thinking about going into business to develop the skills necessary to run that business before going into it. In the case of a hardware business, for instance, I'd advise interested entrepreneurs to work at hardware outlets such as 'Servistar' or others for at least six months prior to striking out on one's own. Many new products come into the market and one has to stay abreast of the latest products and demand in the hardware business. Finally, I underscore the importance of location; it is all about location, location, location."

Yeshimebet (Tutu) Belay
President & CEO
Ethiopian Yellow Pages Advertising
Washington, DC

Yeshimebet (Tutu) Belay was born in 1962 in Jijjiga, a small town in southeastern Ethiopia where the Ogaden region begins. She was raised, however, in Dire Dawa, a commercial and industrial center located on the Addis Ababa-Djibouti railroad. Until 1974, her father, Fitawrari Tesfaye Wondmagnehu, was a provincial governor in different parts of Harrarighe in the southeastern region of Ethiopia.

The small town of Jijjiga was not exactly a seedbed for entrepreneurship, but fortunately, Dire Dawa was and Yeshimebet's latent entrepreneurial talents blossomed in its vibrant commercial atmosphere. Indeed, there were early signs that Yeshimebet would become a full-fledged entrepreneur one day, but no one could have predicted that she would wind up as a pioneering entrepreneur in America.

As a teenager, Yeshimebet fought hard to unleash her entrepreneurial spirit. Her father, as a prominent local governor, never imagined that his daughter would become a businesswoman; rather, she was expected to become a doctor, or lawyer. She also wanted this for herself, at first. In fact, she came to the U.S. as a student to study medicine, but that ambition soon gave way to her desire to become an entrepreneur.

Defying traditional values and social expectations, she followed her heart and embarked upon and embraced an entrepreneurial career. Doing so was out of the norm because Ethiopian culture doesn't place a premium on entrepreneurship, much less for a woman and one of relatively high birth.

Yeshimebet was born into the nobility through her mother's lineage. At the time, royalty clearly had its privileges. In addition to land grants, the Emperor also granted political offices and Yeshimebet's father was appointed to the position of Governor. Although a renowned lawyer in his own right, he became a beneficiary of the patronage system by virtue of his marriage to Yeshimebet's mother. Presumably had Yeshimebet not been "a born entrepreneur," and had the 1974 Revolution not occurred, she could have relied on her social class to land her in a position of relative comfort and ease.

However, her royal lineage is not something Yeshimebet usually talks about. In fact, few people in her social circle know about it, and she chooses not to trade on it in any way. As a practical matter, it should also be noted that since the 1974 revolution, there has been no business advantage associated with belonging to the royal class. The only reason she mentions her family background is to put her upbringing in context, and to underscore the improbability of her choosing an entrepreneurial path, given that entrepreneurship was not held in esteem, especially by the royal class.

Creating an Advantage

Despite of her social background Yeshimebet has always had an eye for business since she was teenager. She saw many business opportunities around her as her family moved from one area to another following her father's various appointments as provincial governor. It was in Dire Dawa, however, that Yeshimebet's entrepreneurial spirit came into full force.

Dire Dawa is one of Ethiopia's major commercial and industrial centers, which is located on the Addis Ababa–Djibouti railroad. Founded in 1902 when the railroad from Djibouti reached the area, its growth has resulted largely from the export and import trade brought by the railroad. The famous Harare coffee, *Khat*, and fruits and vegetables are among Ethiopia's products that are exported from Dire Dawa. The city's importance as a commercial center has grown over time. As a commercial hub in the southeastern part of Ethiopia, it draws people of all backgrounds, including Europeans, Arabs, Indians, and others. This exposed Yeshimebet to different cultures at an early age, and this was important.

"What I found particularly exciting about growing up in Dire Dawa was my interaction with the Afar people who traveled there to meet their chiefs. The vast majority of the Afar population, perhaps 80 percent or more of whom are nomads, have lived life the same way for century upon century; therefore, it was particularly rewarding for me to have my first entrepreneurial breakthrough with the nomads of the Afar region. I don't know how many women in the Afar Region have the possibility of earning and keeping their own money, but for me, one of my motivations for getting into business was the independence that money would bring."

A Lemonade Stand and a New Stand in Life

While life did not deal her lemons personally, she nevertheless had to break new ground and go out into the environment, deal with lemons, and make lemonade. What was the tradition for girls growing up in Ethiopia during the 1970s? In brief, as in other traditional societies, a woman's worth was measured primarily in terms of her role as a mother and wife, and decidedly not in terms of her prowess in business. Not surprisingly, therefore, when Yeshimebet decided to embark on her first entrepreneurial endeavor, she hid it from her family, knowing that it was not befitting a girl of her social class.

Yeshimebet's father's opinion mattered to her and he was her role model. This is not to say that my mother did not have any influence on her, she said, but she looked up to my father. She said, "While my father definitely would not have preferred me to choose a career as an entrepreneur, at the same time, he always told me that I could do anything I wanted to do, which helped me to build confidence in my ability; it gave me the freedom to make my own choices and to believe in my own judgment."

Befitting or not, Yeshimebet could not suppress her entrepreneurial drive. Specifically, what catalyzed her into entrepreneurial action was the opportunity to sell "lemonade" to the Afar people, who came to Dire Dawa to pay tribute and to seek justice from their chief, who lived across the street from her house. They would line up at the compound of the chief's house to wait their turn for an audience with their chief. As they waited and waited for hours on end, they became hungry and thirsty no doubt, Yeshimebet imagined, so the idea to sell them something to eat and drink became an irresistible temptation. "Sometimes, I would make *Embetito* (vegetable or meat dumplings), tomato sandwiches, or egg sandwiches, to sell them," she said. It didn't matter that she was only in primary school and a mere 13 years old; there was a business opportunity to seize, and she seized it.

Handling the logistics of this business while having to hide her involvement in it from her family represented her first management challenge. She solved her problem by drafting other neighborhood girls into service for her new business, despite the fact that they too had to face similar cultural restrictions that discouraged them from being entrepreneurial. The fact that they eagerly joined together with her in this business gives testimony to the importance of leadership, and also to irrepressibility of the latent entrepreneurial sprit among girls.

Yeshimebet now had a 'crew,' and her first line of business was selling sandwiches. Aside from bankrolling the operation, Yeshimebet rose early in the morning each day, bought bread from a nearby bakery, and prepared the sandwiches, which her 'crew' sold at the line in front of the chief's house. At the end of each day, the money was counted and sales commissions were given to the 'crew.' This was her first experience in money management, which later came in handy later.

As her lemonade business continued to grow there came a time when Yeshimebet could no longer hide it from her family. "My first 'lemonade stand' business grew to a scale where I could no longer hide it from my family, at which point my father realized that I had the potential to deviate from the future plans he envisioned for me, she said. While he was no doubt surprised by my actions, he decided not to be unduly worried, because I continued to keep up my grades in school, and that was the most important thing." Yeshimebet adds, "This is not to imply that my parents considered it to be a good thing that I was out there on a 'street corner' selling sandwiches to passers-by. However, in the end, we struck a compromise: As long as I performed well in school, I could continue with my little business activities."

As the business took off, Yeshimebet decided to expand her product range to include fruit juices. Drawing on the resources at her disposal, she took advantage of Dire Dawa's abundant fruit crops, mangoes in particular, and expanded the range of her offerings to include mango juice. With her growing savings, she purchased a juice maker from Addis Ababa, which was her first import. This positive first experience in business left a good 'taste in her mouth' for business, and laid the foundation for her future as a successful businesswoman in America. She also believes that her childhood experience has helped her to develop good communication and marketing skills.

The American Dream

Yeshimebet wasn't a complete rebel. In the end, she decided to follow the career path her father had laid out for her. "As my father wished, I eventually decided to pursue a career as a medical doctor, in the U.S.."

When I finished high school in 1979 and passed the matriculation exam for entering college, I won a scholarship to study in Cuba. While it was an honor to have won the scholarship, I really didn't want to go to Cuba. My dream was to go to the United States. At the time, however, it just was not the 'done thing' to refuse a government scholarship, and I faced a dilemma; should I go against the grain and refuse the scholarship, or just go to Cuba? I consulted my father, who advised me to follow my own heart." Fortunately, the dilemma was resolved for her: It turns out that there was opposition to her selection, and to that of her two colleagues, because they were from 'reactionary' families, so the school decided to withdraw the offer, and Yeshimebet was spared from having to make the choice. Things worked out for Yeshimebet, and she was able to come to United States after all. A year after the Cuba opportunity fell through in 1980, she was able to secure sponsorship from a family in Houston, Texas that allowed her to study in America.

She remembers, "When I first traveled to America, I stayed with my sponsor's family in Houston for about six months, and subsequently moved to Baton Rouge, Louisiana because my female cousin lived there. For the first year, I studied biology at Baton Rouge College to prepare myself for a career in medicine. After a year, however, I switched to majoring in marketing because I realized that it would be too expensive to pursue medicine, as it was, I already had to hold down so many odd jobs to pay my tuition fees and to cover my living expenses," Yeshimebet, said. I worked as house cleaner, sold 'Mary Kay' (cosmetics), worked in stores, and as baby sitter over the years," she recalls.

"Switching my major from medicine to marketing, was a logical choice for me given that many of the jobs I took involved selling and marketing." As Yeshimebet reflects on her life, she believes her background growing up in Dire Dawa prepared her for life in America. As she states, "I was used to foreigners, and to experiencing different cultures, therefore, when I came to America, despite the financial hardships I endured, I embraced the experience fully, and my excitement about being in America never diminished, even when things were not going well. My belief in America as a land of opportunity never wavered."

Resurrection of the Entrepreneurial Spirit

Although in school, Yeshimebet found that she could not hold herself back and defer her real dream of going into business. She remembers, "When I graduated in 1985, instead of looking for a job like most of my classmates, I decided to start my own business. The positive experience I had in running my own business when I was growing up in Dire Dawa, and the sales experience while in college, encouraged me, and I knew I could be successful in business."

"While in college, besides the sales job that I held, I made time to attend seminars and workshops on how to start a business," she said. "What I found to be particularly inspirational was the opportunity to hear from successful businesspersons who shared their stories about how they succeeded in their businesses. My experience as a sales person also gave me confidence to start my own business. I remember when I was working in the Mary Kay cosmetic business, for instance. I was a star salesperson because I never feared rejection. I reckoned that if you are good at marketing, and you are not afraid of rejection, you can always succeed. The key thing is belief in oneself and a positive attitude, which have always been among my strongest personal assets," Yeshimebet noted.

What makes entrepreneurs special is their insights and imagination, which allows them to perceive opportunities where others can't see them. Yeshimebet qualifies as such an entrepreneur, and proved so when she moved to Washington, DC in 1989. No sooner than she moved to Washington, she spotted an opportunity that no one else had previously spotted. With the growing population of Ethiopian immigrants in the Washington metropolitan area, Yeshimebet saw an emerging demand from them for information about groceries, restaurants, clinics, law offices, real estates, insurances, and other services that were geared to their needs. What she had stumbled upon was the idea for her new business: An Ethiopian Yellow Pages.

"When I first struck upon the idea of publishing an Ethiopian Yellow Pages," Yeshimebet explains, "My goal was to provide a service, rather than of focusing on making money. I was keen to discover who everyone was in the community, and delighted in meeting Ethiopian lawyers, insurance and real estate brokers, dentists, doctors, community organizations, residential and business loan financiers, churches, and others. It soon turned into a business idea, however." Once it turned into business ensure that she identified and included a broad range of Ethiopian-owned businesses, churches, community organizations, and other entities that serviced the Ethiopian community.

Yeshimebet wasn't sure if the response to her request for them to advertise would be positive, but it was. She said, "The Ethiopian business community embraced the idea and were very supportive; they provided their information and feedback, and paid me in advance." The first Ethiopian Yellow Pages rolled off the press in 1993, but it had taken Yeshimebet almost three years from the time she first conceived the idea. The first edition contained about 80 pages and 1,000 copies were printed. Today, Ethiopian Yellow Pages contains over 600 pages, and the print run is over several thousand copies.

Yeshimebet underscores that that the development of first Yellow Pages was challenging; it did not happen overnight. "From the inception of the idea, to actually producing the Yellow Pages took three years took a great deal of time. It was no small feat to gather information about the growing number of Ethiopians entities in the Washington Metropolitan area. "I had to collect the information by myself, as I had no staff and no previous reference documents upon which to draw," Yeshimebet said.

The participation of her family in the business lightened her load, however. Yeshimebet is quick to credit her family's role in her business, and in her success, noting, "While I did the lion's share of information collection, my family played an invaluable role in developing the business. My husband, brothers, and sisters all helped in different ways to support the business. I also owe a debt of gratitude to the many members of the Ethiopian community who supported my idea, many of whom reached into their pockets and gave me a check on the spot, which enabled me to keep going until the publication was completed."

Yeshimebet especially acknowledges her husband's support, noting, "When I started the Ethiopian Yellow Pages, my husband Yehune, and I were already married, and from the beginning, he has been key to the success of our business. The design and editorial work of the first two publications were done with outside help, but from the third publication onwards, Yehune took over. He is now in charge of the design and publication of the Ethiopian Yellow Pages. Initially, he used Microsoft Publisher, and before long, he graduated to more advanced publishing software such as Quark, Express, Photoshop Illustrator, and Freehand. We now also have graphic designers who work with him. His support and involvement in the business is not only important for his technical contributions; he is also my emotional support, my friend, as well as my partner."

A Little Help from Family and Friends

The money to establish a business has to come from somewhere. Yeshimebet says that in her case, financing came from advertising sales, and from her own personal savings. She adds, "As I started the business from home, the overhead costs were low. In addition, as my husband and I lived with my brothers and sisters, and my siblings were drafted into service to support the business in various ways. In this sense, you can say my brothers and sisters gave us indirect financial contributions."

"The fact that my family has been involved in the business has enabled me to expand into new areas. For instance, we now provide a phone information service to our clients. You can say we are the "411" of the Ethiopian community in our area. We also get calls from outside the U.S. requesting information about Ethiopians in various communities. Our business continues to grow, and we get many referrals from our customers. When the economy slows down, you would expect that advertisement budgets to shrink, but to the contrary, our business continues to grow."

Never one to rest on her laurels, Yeshimebet says that she continues to try new businesses. For instance, she remembers, "We organized a two-day Ethiopian Expo in 2003, to showcase the products and services of Ethiopian suppliers, and to introduce them to buyers from the community at large that are interested in the Ethiopian community. The idea started quite simply: since we already had a network of many businesses and social organizations through our Yellow Pages, it was a logical next step to introduce them to each other. Prior to organizing the Expo, we used to host business networking events at the Madison Hotel. We did this over a four-year period, and built a constituency. Soon we became the 'go-to' source for such matchmaking."

Yeshimebet's Ethio Expo 2003 was a resounding success and many deals were consummated. "The Expo attracted several thousands of visitors, and was covered by all the Amharic radio stations in the Metropolitan area," Yeshimebet said. "I even heard that Ethiopian Television in Ethiopia aired the event. The event was not only a success in terms of achieving its objectives, it also served to promote our Yellow Pages as well," Yeshimebet added. Her goal is to expand the event. At the time this book was sent for publication, Yeshimebet had already hosted a successful 2004 Ethio Expo, for the third consecutive year.

Yeshimebet doesn't want anyone to think that a successful business is all smooth sailing, because it isn't. She underscores that there is always the constant challenge of collecting receivables. "In the advertisement business," according to Yeshimebet, "the client pays half upfront, and the balance when the publication is printed, which means that there is always work to be done in collecting one's receivables. Some of our clients may also have large accounts which means that the Ethiopian Yellow Pages has a steady flow of work throughout the year."

Breaking New Ground

Being a trailblazer is never easy, as Yeshimebet's experience confirms. "The fact that we published the first Ethiopian Yellow Pages in the area meant that we had a major mountain to climb sell the idea to advertisers. What I learned in the process is that you don't know who will say yes, and who will say no, until you ask. I had to identify my target customers, talk to them about my business idea, and convince them that they would get the value of their money if they advertised in my publication," she reflects.

Ensuring the quality of the publication was yet another challenge for Yeshimebet. "As an advertisement publication the quality has to be up to the standard. This required me to reinvest a significant portion of my profits back into the business in the first few years."

There were further challenges she had to face. "No matter what kind of product you may have, if you can't distribute it to the targeted market there is no value to it." Therefore, Yeshimebet explains, "A great deal of my initial effort was focused on figuring out distribution strategies. This entailed attending many events, such as church events, social gatherings, weddings, and others to market the publication. If there were eleven weddings in the Washington Metropolitan area, I would attend all eleven of them to distribute the Ethiopian Yellow Pages to each guest individually."

As the first and the only publisher of the Ethiopian Yellow Pages, Yeshimebet also has other concerns. She recalls how afraid she was about the whole notion of advertising and the responsibilities that came with it. "The greatest fear associated with advertising is whether the product really delivers what advertisers expect. At the same time, you want to ensure that their expectations are reasonable, because if they are not used to advertising, and expect quick results, they will be disappointed. Therefore, it is important to educate new advertisers about what to expect from advertising. At the same time, I also have to be concerned about getting new clients, while maintaining the old ones.

Measures of Success

According to Yeshimebet, one measure of the success of her business is the increasing number of entries in the directory, which on the one hand reflects the growth of the Ethiopian community in Washington, DC, and on the other, her ability to capture them in her directory. "We estimate that we cover up to 80 percent of the Ethiopian-owned businesses in the Washington Metropolitan area. In addition, we have a growing number of non-Ethiopian owned businesses, who have also become regular customers."

There is a balance she must strike: Developing a loyal customer base, while increasing her clientele. On the one hand, we have to bring in new clients every year, but at the same time we have to be able to keep our existing clients, which means that we have to make sure they are getting value for their money. If existing clients are dissatisfied with our service, if our publication isn't good enough, and our distribution network is not wide enough to reach a broad network of social and business organizations, then we would not be able to stay in business. If we succeed in bringing 20 percent new customers on the one hand, while losing 30 percent of our existing clients, there would be a net loss in our clientele base." It is a tricky business.

In comparing how her business fares compared to other similar businesses, she notes, "When I look into the trends of many ethnic advertisement publications in our area, many of them are getting thinner every year, because many of their clients drop out. The hallmark of a good advertisement publication is bringing new clients every year without losing the existing clientele base. Our goal is to earn customer loyalty by ensuring the quality of our publication, by developing effective distribution outlets, and by expanding our outreach within our target community. Consequently, many of our clients have been with us for a long time and are willing to pay more to get a premium spot in our publication. For instance, any one of our clients on the cover would pay even triple the current fee to be on the front cover. At the same time, we have several clients waiting for the prime spots in our publication. On balance, in the past eleven years, the Ethiopian Yellow Pages has shown a steady growth and strong customer loyalty."

Lessons for the Novice

"The key to success in any endeavor is to have a positive outlook and to be optimistic. My mother's favorite prayer was, *'God, give me the ability to love and to be loved by people.'* This prayer has guided me throughout my life. Indeed, without the kindness of so many people, I could not have I achieved what I have in my life. I advise emerging entrepreneurs to develop their social capital and to strive to be innovative, focus on what they do best, develop their skills, and plan ahead. I particularly stress the importance of having a unique product and service. The Ethiopian Yellow Pages is an example of this."

"As with any new idea, you will always have naysayers, people who do not believe that your idea will work, just because they have never seen it before. Some of my family members fell into this category. I remember having a brainstorming session with one of my brothers who was very skeptical about the viability of the yellow pages idea. In order to convince him, I had to come up with a simple strategy. I took a piece of paper and created a category of possible responses to my idea. One category consisted of those who would most likely say "no," the second category included the "may-be(s)", and the third category was the "yes" people. We took this list and drove around Washington DC, and contacted minority businesses to ask them to advertise in our Ethiopian Yellow Pages. Our first attempt was with a Cuban-American businessman; we expected him to say no. Sure enough, when we asked him if he would advertise in a forthcoming Ethiopian Yellow Pages, his response was 'no.' But, we continued contacting firms on the next few blocks, and found that some of those who we thought would not be interested were positive. Then, I told my brother, "If people who we expected to show no interest in our product are interested, then we should not be afraid of failing because we know that many businesses, both in our own community and outside of it, can see the value of an Ethiopian Yellow Pages.""

When I started out, all I had was my idea and my ability to develop a strategy for marketing. This was all I needed, as it turned out. I attribute my success to the combination of a good idea and good marketing. I cannot overemphasize the importance of mastering the art of communication. Any good idea is only as good as people think it is; therefore, it is imperative to be able to effectively communicate its benefits and merits."

"Securing one's family support is another key pillar and foundation upon which to build a business. In my case, my husband's unwavering support and direct contribution has contributed significantly to the success of our business. As we started this business from our home, it was particularly important to have the backing of my husband. Furthermore, there were many occasions when I had to go out and sell the product, and to attend social events that took me away from home. Had my husband not been supportive, it never would have worked.

Finally, I also wish to underscore the importance of garnering community support. Without the support of the Ethiopian business community, I would not be where I am now. The Ethiopian Yellow Pages, as a business, wouldn't have grown without community support.

Haile Sadik
Proprietor and Manager
Autorent, Inc.
Brentwood, Maryland

B orn in 1958 in Zalambessa, Haile Sadik has come a long way from a childhood in northern Ethiopia, where there were few automobiles, all the way to America where he now owns Autorent Inc., a car rental business with five employees and gross revenues of over half a million dollars per year. Not only did Haile make it to America against all odds, he blazed a new trail in business as the first Ethiopian in the Washington, DC metropolitan area to own a car dealership.

Haile's family struggled to make ends meet when he was growing up. His maternal grandmother raised him after his parents divorced. His grandmother barely had enough resources to keep him fed and clothed and the situation worsened when his mother, whom he scarcely knew during the 14 years that he was raised by his grandmother, divorced yet again and returned to live with her mother, bringing two more younger sisters, Werku and Shewaye, to join the crowded household.

"Sometimes the only food we had to eat was *koointi* (tuber), which is the fleshy part of an underground root," Haile recalls. "My mother and sisters used to dig up tuber for hours in order to extract enough of the root to make a meal out of it. To get three or four pounds to roast for dinner took many hours of digging."

Going to school was a big challenge under the circumstances. "My mother had to send me weekly food rations despite her limited resources," Haile remembers. "Sometimes she could only send *besso* (roasted barley flour)." These meager rations, Haile adds, "meant that sometimes my mother and my younger sisters had to skip meals so that I could go to school." It was a hard life. "Life became so difficult that when I was eighteen years old, I had to move out and live with one of my aunts because there simply was not enough food to go around," he said. "As the situation steadily worsened, my sisters also had to move on to a place called Irob, where they could live on cactus pears during the summer." To say it was a hard life is an understatement in Haile's case. Yet, as he explains, "I was lucky to be able to complete high school under the circumstances, but even luckier to be able to move to the United States in 1981."

Completing high school was a major feat for Haile no doubt but his enthusiasm for education was never daunted: He believed that education could transform his life. "As a child," Haile explains, "I couldn't accept the kind of life my mother, sisters, and I were leading; I knew there had to be a better life I could live somehow, somewhere."

When Haile started elementary school in Sebeya, a town adjacent to Zalambessa, in 1967, he began to imagine a different future, one where people lived better lives, where there was food on the table, where people had money in their pockets and hope in their hearts. "I, too, wanted to lead such a life," Haile said. "Going to school," he said, "was a godsend: Sitting behind a desk and being exposed to new information and new realms of possibility created an excitement in me I had never felt before. It gave me my first glimpse of a better world and made me believe education was a path out of poverty." In 1979, Haile completed high school and in 1980, he was admitted to Addis Ababa University. As his mother and siblings needed his help, however, he had no choice but to drop out to take a job as a librarian closer to home.

From the Inside Out

Haile realized how important education was and the role that it plays in instilling something in people that gives them the strength to change their lives. He also realized from firsthand experience just how debilitating and consuming abject poverty could be and how it can rob a person of the strength to create the catalyst for change. He explained, "Take my mother's case, for instance, I remember how she used to carry heavy loads of hay on her back from a village more than seven miles away from Sebeya to feed our two oxen, which were our only assets. Did she want to change her life? Absolutely, but there was limited opportunity for her to do so".

"The land tenure situation," for instance, Haile notes, "played a role in limiting the opportunities for women, in particular. As land was communally owned, when my mother returned to her family after her second marriage failed, she was entitled to a piece of land in her home area, provided that she lived there. As a single mother, she was eligible for only half the size as would have been allotted to a married couple. Her share was less than two acres, which meant no matter how hard she tried, she would never be able to produce enough to transform her life and improve her fortunes. All she could do was barely survive. The level of poverty we were living in was so deep it was hard to claw our way out. There were times when having *sibko* (watery grits) and *koointi* for dinner was a good day. While my mother's hard work and struggle was not able to transform her own life, her efforts were instrumental in transforming mine, and in enflaming my passion to succeed in life. In fact, I owe my success in life to my mother and uncles, without whose help I wouldn't be where I am now."

At Odds with the Government

Like many other Ethiopian immigrants who have come to the United States, Haile has a story. His story and his struggle in the opposition to the Derg regime began in 1976 when he joined the Tigray Popular Liberation Front (TPLF), which opposed the then Derg regime in Ethiopia. "I joined the TPLF from Sinkata, about 44 miles north of Mekele, the capital of the Tigray Province, where I was assigned as a teacher under the Development through Cooperation Campaign (the *Zemecha)* national service," he explains. After few months, however, Haile decided to drop out because he didn't think the goals and strategies of the organization were consistent with his values.

He was later granted amnesty from the government. For the next five years Haile tried everything in his power to pull himself and his family out of poverty: He finished high school, joined university, and then took a job to help his mother and siblings. As an ex-combatant in the TPLF, however, when the government started rounding up suspected members of the TPLF and throwing them in jail in 1980 without being charged, Haile feared that he would be next. He managed to escape imprisonment and death, but he knew it would only be a matter of time before his luck ran out. So, he decided to take matters in his own hands and make a run for the border. He escaped to Djibouti in 1980, before it was too late; in Djibouti he applied for and succeeded in being granted refugee status to enter the United States.

148

Over the Rainbow

Haile made it "over the rainbow" and landed in the United States in 1981. Unlike many other Ethiopians who arrived in this country at the time under similar circumstances, his expectations about life in America were fairly realistic. As he explains, "Yes, I believed that America was a land of many opportunities, but at the same time I knew I would have to work hard to take advantage of the opportunities offered. I knew it wasn't going to be easy, and I didn't expect anyone to spoon-feed me. I was prepared to work hard and to do whatever was necessary to succeed in my life." Despite his modest goals and expectations, he was disappointed nevertheless.

Haile was particularly disappointed because he had always believed that education would transform his life and now that he had acquired it, it didn't seem to be enough. He had thought that obtaining an education in America would immediately lead to a high paying job. What he found, however, was that it was difficult for an immigrant to break through the job market in America.

In order to pay for school, he worked at Kmart for $3.65 an hour, which enabled him to rent a small room for $100 a month. He also worked at his school in the work-study program, where he earned up to $70 per week, which was also fine. When he earned an associate's degree in electronics from Baltimore Community College's School of Electronics Technology in 1985, he was ready to take off and start living the "real" American dream. Unfortunately, things didn't work out according to plan.

The first shock came when he got a job at an electronic company, working on an assembly line assembling electronic boards. It was grueling and monotonous work. He remembers, "I had to sit in a small station for up to eight hours a day, patiently assembling small parts one after another, I thought I would lose my mind. Day after day, hour after hour, assembling one gadget after another, and all for nine dollars an hour—no, this was not the American dream," Haile said.

Being a blue-collar worker while going to school was one thing, but having to do that after he graduated was quite another. He didn't come all the way to America from his native home to be a blue-collar worker. As he explained, "When I earned my associate degree I expected to get a job making at least $30,000 a year, but I was never able to land a job that paid more than $9 per hour. I was sorely disappointed."

"I became a 'necessity entrepreneur,' one who had no choice but to go into business to earn a decent living," Haile learned, however, that without connections, money, and with little information, the choices of what to do in business were limited. As many Ethiopians had resorted to becoming taxi drivers, Haile investigated that option and decided it could be a steppingstone for him. While there were some barriers to entry in this business, such as the need to obtain a permit, which cost $15,000, and the need to pass an exam on how to drive in the city, the hurdles were not insurmountable and he joined the ranks of so many other Ethiopian taxicab drivers with dreams in waiting.

At first everything worked out fine: He was making good money and he had a degree of independence. As a taxi driver, he made $200 a day, which is more than he had been making. It fell apart quickly, however, when the reality of sitting in a car for up to 15 hours a day struck home. When the reality hit he felt as if he had lost his dignity. When he started to lose his sense of self worth, he knew it was time to change his life yet again.

A New Day Dawns

One always needs a bit of luck, and finally Haile got lucky. His luck came when he ran into a car dealer he had known previously. A few years back, Haile had bought his first car from this dealer. When they met again, the car dealer asked Haile to drive cars from an auction site and offered to pay him $50 per trip, which was quite a welcome addition to his income. The only problem for Haile was what was an auction? He soon found out it was a way to sell cars to the highest bidders. In 1986, when he attended his first auction in Hartford County, Maryland at the Belair Auction, his life changed. When he saw how one could walk away with great deals and that cars were sold well below their market value, he knew he was on to something. "When I saw what the car dealer was doing, I said to myself, if he could do it, I could do it." He said, "It immediately occurred to me that there were many Ethiopians in need of cars and that if I was able to purchase them at reasonable prices, and then sell them to Ethiopians in need, I could make a business out of it, which is what I did."

A Car Dealership Is Born

Haile's first car dealership consisted of purchasing cars from the auction and selling them to Ethiopians. It was a home-based business; he didn't need premises because he took orders from his friends and delivered the cars to them at their doorstep after he purchased them at the auction. He did this for two years while he continued to drive his taxi on weekdays. When the business grew to the point that he felt confident about leaving the taxi business, a new car dealership was born.

Once he took the leap, it became important to grow the business, as he could no longer rely on his taxicab. The first thing he did was formalize his business by incorporating it; then he leased a lot from which he could sell his cars. With the $18,000 he had saved from driving taxicabs and selling cars on the side, he leased a lot at 928 Euclid Street in Washington, DC, and opened his first car dealership there in 1990. He chose the location because of its proximity to the Adams Morgan and U Street areas where many Ethiopian-owned businesses are concentrated. At the time, he notes, "the monthly rate for open lots was very cheap and I was paying $300 a month, which helped me to operate at minimum overhead cost." His next step was to advertise in the Yellow Pages. Advertising alone cost upwards of $4,000 per year, but it paid off and his business did well for the next five years; it did so well that he had to acquire a bigger location.

The progression from taxicab driver, to home-based business owner, to car dealer may seem easy, but it wasn't a simple path. It is hard to convey the magnitude and severity of the challenges immigrants like Haile have to face as entrepreneurs. As he explains, "I had to overcome financial constraints and language barriers, and also build a social network. Most importantly, I had to overcome the fear I had of failure and operating in a foreign environment. It was hard going, but I was determined to succeed, because I knew what real poverty was and I never wanted to be in that state again."

Once You Get Started...

There is no time for fear and apprehension once you get going in a business. The only thing you can do is move forward. In 1996 that is what Haile did when he moved his business to a larger location in Brentwood, Maryland. Strategically located on the edge of Washington, DC, this area appeared to be well positioned to attract customers of all types who come into the area. Haile's decision paid off: His business continued to grow to the point that he was able to double the number of cars he was selling up to 20 cars per month. But as can happen in any business, the good times stopped rolling, and his car sales business started to slow down by 1999. Never one to stagnate, Haile was quick to change with the times.

In 1999, Haile conceived of another business idea, which was renting cars instead of selling them. It worked this way according to Haile: "When I purchased the fleet of cars, if I could not sell them, I'd rent them, and keep the cash flow going." It took him some time to build a new client base in the car rental business and to learn the risks associated with leasing cars versus selling them. The main difference he found was that when you sell the car unless something is wrong with it, you are finished with it, but when you lease it, there are many responsibilities and liabilities one has to take on. The risks of car damage, car theft, and accidents are always looming in the car rental business, he points out. The implication of this is much higher insurance premiums, which increases the cost of doing business. "On the positive side, as compared with selling cars, there are more repeat customers in the rental business," Haile adds.

As with any business, there are always challenges. "The key challenge is maintaining the quality of our service," Haile says. "I have developed my car rental business on three foundations: quality customer service, competitive price, and on accepting cash as a form of payment. It is very important that each and every customer is treated well and gets our full attention when he or she patronizes our business."

The formula seems to be working, because Haile's business continues to expand. He has opened two new locations: Oxen Hill and Silver Spring, Maryland. He has come a long way from being a person who knew little about engines and transmissions to one who buys and sells cars. As he says, "I don't have to know how to fix a car: I just have to know where to find the right person who will."

When Haile started out, he had purchased a number of cars that had faulty engines and transmissions. "My losses due to such errors totaled $17,000 in the first year of my business, and my financial position was unattractive to banks, especially since I didn't have a house or other property I could post for collateral." Although Haile knew about the U.S. Small Business Administration (SBA), he didn't think it would lend him money because he didn't have any substantial business experience. He says he was scared to get a loan guarantee from the government because he feared that if his business failed, he might get in to trouble with the government. In retrospect, he explains, "Since I started out, I have gotten smarter in the process and have also improved my financial position, which enables me to purchase better cars. My credit record wasn't so good at first, but little by little I improved my credit and now I can access all the financing I need. I am also careful to maintain a good credit score."

Advice to Emerging Business Owners

"Change comes from within. If one has a clear goal and motivation, and works hard, he can change his circumstances and his dreams can come true," Haile says. "I continue to dream bigger and bigger dreams and am confident that I will be able to make them come true, especially with the continued and loving support of my wife, who has stood by my side and stayed at home to ensure that our two children have a solid foundation upon which to move forward. I'd also advise my Ethiopian compatriots to learn from the way business is done by others; we don't have to always start from scratch in our learning. Finally, my advice is to realize that money doesn't bring happiness: Happiness comes from within and from believing in oneself.

Epilogue

Ethiopian Americans are part of the larger community of immigrants who are helping to reshape America through their visions and actions, and who are contributing substantially to the American economy through their successful entrepreneurship. Although relatively new comers to America, and small compared to other larger immigrant communities, Ethiopians in the United States have been making strides in academia, business, and in various professions. Their successes are particularly noteworthy, as they have come from a country with limited resources, and limited entrepreneurial traditions.

The interviewees in this book have shared their words of wisdom, and have advised emerging entrepreneurs on how to avoid the pitfalls in business and how to craft winning strategies. Some of the important lessons learned from these conversations are summarized below.

Social and family background matters. Their stories show how they were able to draw strength from their backgrounds while transforming themselves, and how they remain Ethiopian while retaining their social, and cultural traditions. In short, their experience shows us how it is possible to have the best of both worlds.

Their experience also shows that although many came as refuges and asylum seekers, and others came to pursue professions that didn't pan out, they were resilient enough to take advantage of opportunities that presented themselves and which they created. It proves that given the right enabling environment, entrepreneurs will emerge, even when they don't have an entrepreneurial background.

Ethiopians are good savers, is another conclusion that can be drawn from the interviewees in this book. Virtually all of them saved the money that they needed to finance their own start up business. Some of them also relied on each other for financing, which is typical of many newcomer immigrants. They, like others before them, tend to seek external financing for growth, rather than for start up capital.

Family support also matters. The interviewees typically relied on the support of family and friends, and are quick to underscore the importance of building social capital in one's own community, as well as in others. They actively participate in trade associations and business networks, and they serve their community and are an integral part of the community.

Hard work is another theme that ran throughout their stories. But not just hard work: Smart hard work that is directed by clear goals and vision.

Consulting people in the know is yet another important piece of advice that most of the interviewees gave. They also underscore the importance of doing one's own homework to verify the information one gets. Knowing one's target market, identifying and securing the right location, and developing the right business plan, are also key ingredients for success.

Having experience in the business one wants to start is advice given across the board. The key is by working in the business before venturing into entrepreneurship, one not only gets firsthand experience about the business, it positions one not to be so dependent on their employees for information.

Prudent financial planning and management is yet another trait shared by all of the successful entrepreneurs in the book. They caution that whereas there are many things that one wants to buy; one must have the self-discipline to delay gratification in order to build wealth.

The profit goal, they note, is not "the goal." Although a motivating factor in business, their experiences suggest that profit alone is not ultimately what motivates them to work hard. As one of the interviewees commented, "once you achieve a certain financial return, and a certain comfort level, accumulating additional wealth stops being a motivating factor. The fun is in the idea of creating a business. It is the desire to create something new and to succeed in what one does that motivates people."

Because of their hard work, persistence, and business acumen, these first generation Ethiopian immigrants have made their dreams come true, and in the process, they have created job opportunities for themselves and for many others from their community and outside of it as well. Collectively, the interviewees in this book employ hundreds of workers and have generated millions of dollars in revenues, and paid their fair share of taxes.

Coming as students and refugees, they are surprised to be living the American dream. If they can do it, you can do it too.

REFERENCES

Brockhaus, R. H. (1989). *The Psychology of the entrepreneur.* In Kent, C. A., Sexton, D. L., & Vesper, K. H. (Eds.), *Encyclopedia of Entrepreneurship.* Englewood Cliffs, New Jersey: Prentice-Hall, Inc.

Hayton, J. C., George, G., & Zahra, S. A. (2002). National Culture and Entrepreneurship: A review of research. *Entrepreneurship Theory and Practice. Summer 2002,* 33-52. Retrieved June 24, 2003, from Business Source Premier.

Hosler, A. S. (1998). *Japanese Immigrant Entrepreneurs in New York City: A new wave of ethnic business.* New York: Garland Publishers

Korten, D. C. (1972). *Planned Change in a Transitional Society: Psychological Problems of Modernization in Ethiopia.* New York: Praeger Publishers.

Light, I., & Bonacich, E. (1988). *Immigrant Entrepreneurs: Koreans in Los Angeles, 1965–1982.* Berkeley: University of California Press.

Light, I., Georges, S., Mehdi, B., & Claudia, D. (1994). Beyond the Ethnic Enclave Economy. *Social Problems,* 41, 65-80.

Metaferia, G., & Shifferraw, M. (1991). *The Ethiopian Revolution of 1974 and The Exodus of Ethiopia's Trained Human Resources.* African Studies, Vol. 24.: The Edwin Mellon Press.

Mengistea, T. (2001). Indigenous ethnicity and entrepreneurial success in Africa: Some evidence from Ethiopia. *Policy Research Working Paper, No. 2534,* Washington, DC: The World Bank.

Ottaway, M., & Ottaway, D. (1978). *Ethiopia, Empire in Revolution.* New York: Africana Publishing Company

Pankhurst, R. (1990). A Social History of Ethiopia. Addis Ababa University.

Sanders, J. M., & Nee, V. (1996). Immigrant self-employment: the family as social capital and the value of human capital. *American Sociological Review,* 61, 231–49.

Singer, A., Friedman, S., Cheung I., & Price, M. (2001). *The world in a zip code: Greater Washington, D.C. as a new region of immigration.* Washington, DC: The Brookings Institution.

U.S. Government Printing Office (1997, 1998, 2002). <u>Statistical Year Book of Immigration and Naturalization Services</u>. Washington, D.C.: Author.

Waldinger, R., Aldrich, H., Ward, R., & Associates. (1990) *Ethnic Entrepreneurs: Immigrant Business in Industrial Societies.* Newbury Park, CA: Sage Publications.

How to Order Books by AASBEA Publishers

By Credit Card: www.AASBEA.COM

By Direct Purchase: Mail check to:

PETER H. GEBRE   2300 M Street, NW, Suite 800
Washington, DC 20037
Email: info@aasbea.com
Web: www.aasbea.com

Other Books By AASBEA Publishers:

Mail Check to: "AASBEA"

- *African Leaders Reach Out to Africans in the Diaspora* (Freeman, 2004)

- *Conversations With Powerful African Women Leaders: Inspiration, Motivation, and Strategy* (Freeman, 2002)

- *Recipes From the Road: Favorite Global Recipes of Washington, DC's Global Women* (Freeman, 2002)

- *Exporting, Importing, and E-Commerce: A "How To" Guide For Minority, Immigrant and Women-Owned Firms* (Freeman, 2001)

- *Conversations With Women Who Export: Inspiration, Motivation, and Strategy* (Freeman, 2000)

Some also available on Amazon.com